Cricket

99.94 Tips to Improve Your Game

Ken Davis

Neil Buszard

Human Kinetics

Library of Congress Cataloging-in-Publication Data

Davis, Ken, 1946-
  Cricket : 99.94 tips to improve your game / Ken Davis and Neil Buszard.
    p. cm.
  ISBN-13: 978-0-7360-9078-0 (soft cover)
  ISBN-10: 0-7360-9078-9 (soft cover)
  1. Cricket--Training. I. Buszard, Neil, 1953- II. Title.
  GV917.D38 2011
  796.358--dc22

                              2010052854

  ISBN-10: 0-7360-9078-9 (print)
  ISBN-13: 978-0-7360-9078-0 (print)

The players' statistics cited in this text can be found at www.espncricinfo.com and were current as of March, 2011.

Acquisitions Editor: Peter Murphy; **Developmental Editor:** Anne Hall; **Assistant Editor:** Tyler Wolpert; **Copyeditor:** Joy Wotherspoon; **Graphic Designer:** Joe Buck; **Graphic Artist:** Julie L. Denzer; **Cover Designer:** Keith Blomberg; **Photographer (cover):** Hamish Blair/Getty Images; **Printer:** Versa Press

Human Kinetics books are available at special discounts for bulk purchase. Special editions or book excerpts can also be created to specification. For details, contact the Special Sales Manager at Human Kinetics.

Printed in the United States of America   10 9 8 7 6 5 4 3 2 1

The paper in this book is certified under a sustainable forestry program.

Human Kinetics
Web site: www.HumanKinetics.com

United States: Human Kinetics
P.O. Box 5076
Champaign, IL 61825-5076
800-747-4457
e-mail: humank@hkusa.com

Canada: Human Kinetics
475 Devonshire Road Unit 100
Windsor, ON N8Y 2L5
800-465-7301 (in Canada only)
e-mail: info@hkcanada.com

Europe: Human Kinetics
107 Bradford Road
Stanningley
Leeds LS28 6AT, United Kingdom
+44 (0) 113 255 5665
e-mail: hk@hkeurope.com

Australia: Human Kinetics
57A Price Avenue
Lower Mitcham, South Australia 5062
08 8372 0999
e-mail: info@hkaustralia.com

New Zealand: Human Kinetics
P.O. Box 80
Torrens Park, South Australia 5062
0800 222 062
e-mail: info@hknewzealand.com

E5078

Contents

Foreword

Sir Donald (Don) Bradman and the figure 99.94 are well entrenched in cricket folklore and synonymous with each other. Bradman is statistically the greatest cricketer to ever play the game. His batting average of 99.94 is still almost twice as good as anyone else who has played Test cricket. Therefore, it makes sense that a book written about cricket for coaches and players should include 99 chapters.

Neil Buszard and Ken Davis have been playing and coaching cricket for the past 40 years. As leaders in the game, they challenge convention to create better players and a better game.

This book is not a typical instructional manual. It is filled with a variety of views and strategies to help both athletes and coaches improve their game. It provides useful tips and generates critical thinking. For some, the points will merely crystallize thoughts. For others, they may open minds to a much broader appreciation of the game than just the basics.

If you are looking for the edge on your competitors or you are in need of some inspiration, *Cricket: 99.94 Tips to Improve Your Game* might be just the catalyst you are seeking.

Merv Hughes

Sir Donald Bradman								
	Matches	Inns	Runs	HS	Ave	100s	50s	Catches
Tests	52	80	6996	334	99.94	29		

Acknowledgments

To my mum, Lorna; and dad, Ken; who nurtured my love for sport and encouraged me throughout my career.

To my children, Rhett, Brooke, and Ben, who inspired me to appreciate the value and fascination of the written word.

To the late George Tribe, who introduced me to the science and art of cricket. His wisdom and smiling face always greeted me after a hot day in the field chasing leather.

To Brian Nettleton, my lecturer at Melbourne University, who showed me how to think creatively about teaching and coaching.

To my brother, Barry, who is a model sportsman, teacher, and a deep thinker about all the sport we have played together. A champion to me and others he has taught and coached.

To all the clubs that showed faith in me as a coach, to the players and colleagues who have provided the environment for me to discover and apply many of the ideas expressed in this book, I am eternally grateful.

To all the team-mates and opponents I've worked with, who have contributed to the lessons I've learned and to a lifetime of wonderful memories.

Ken Davis

To my mum, Gladys; dad, Ernie; and brother, Ian; who have encouraged and supported my love of sport.

To my wife, Liz, who has had to endure the highs and lows of playing and coaching—but has always supported my endeavours.

To my sons, Peter and Tim, who share my passion of sport and inspire others with their dedication to their individual pursuits.

To George Murray and Keith Stackpole, my senior cricket coaches, and Lyn Straw and David Went, my senior baseball coaches, who nurtured my skills and who, in their own ways, provided the foundation for my sporting career.

To Frank Pyke and Peter Spence, of the Victorian Institute of Sport, who helped to develop my coaching philosophy and enhance my personal growth.

To every team-mate, assistant coach, sports scientist and administrative assistant who shared their passion of sport and helped me achieve success.

Neil Buszard

Introduction

This book explores aspects of playing and coaching cricket that do not typically appear in how-to books on the game. Therefore, you will not find much content about the techniques involved in the myriad of batting strokes in a batter's repertoire. You won't learn how to bowl an outswinger, leg-spinner, off-cutter, or even a doosra. However, there is something here for both the elite player and the grass-roots cricketer.

In order to consistently play cricket well, a strong foundation of fundamental skills that will stand up under pressure is needed. However, you must couple this skill with an ever-expanding understanding of the nuances of the game. For instance, you need tactical sense, a focused mind, and the ability to adapt to any situation that confronts you. In short, go beyond the basics in order to excel in the competitive world of cricket.

Through our years of playing, coaching, and learning about cricket, we have gathered insights from a number of sources that can benefit players and coaches alike. We have gained wisdom from fellow players, athletes we have coached, and most importantly, the sport-science researchers with whom we have been involved. This information can set you on the path to cricket excellence. If you follow the concepts outlined in this book, we have no doubt that you will become a better player or coach. We hope your thinking about the sport is challenged and your performance and appreciation of the game is enhanced.

You can pick this book up at any time and read a couple of points. Some tips are longer than others, which reflects both a fundamental difference in our writing styles and the very nature of the game. Some overs take longer than others, some outfielders run more than the slip cordon, and some batters sprint distances that vary from 20 to 60 metres when scoring. Be prepared for diversity!

Our original intent was to compile a century of cricket tips, but we changed that when we thought of the man who took cricket performance to levels that have never been, and probably never will be, emulated. Sir Don Bradman's Test-batting average of 99.94 seemed an apt figure on which to model the number of chapters. We did not see Bradman play, but we have marvelled at his dominance of opposition attacks. His footwork and attacking all-round game would no doubt have allowed him to excel in any era. He is simply the pinnacle of batting craft.

We trust you will enjoy reading the book, whether on the train to work or in the comfort of your own home. We guarantee that heeding the advice will give you as much enjoyment and satisfaction as we get from the game that has meant so much.

Key: Abbreviations used in statistical tables	
Abbreviation	Explanation
HS	Highest score—The highest score an individual has made in a particular format of the game
ODI	One day international—A game played between two countries and consisting of 50 overs per side
ListA	One day games—Limited over games played between first class teams
Twenty20	Twenty over games—Games of 20 overs per side
NO	Not out—An innings played by a batter whereby they were not dismissed
Econ	Economy—The average amount of runs conceded per over bowled
Wkts	Wickets—The number of dismissals a bowler takes
5Wkts	5 wickets in an innings—The number of times a bowler takes 5 or more wickets in an innings
BT Ave	The average (batting)—The average of runs made against innings played
BW Ave	The average (bowling)—The average runs made against the wicket taken

Batting

Batting in cricket is both an art and a science. Artistic players like Brian Lara and Mahela Jayawardene enthral crowds with their graceful movement and exquisite handwork as they thread the ball through the fielder's net. In contrast, scientific batters like Simon Katich and Justin Langer study the type of delivery and field placements to determine the most efficient way of scoring runs within their repertoire of skills. In reality, most elite batters use a measure of both art and science.

Batting caters for the power player and the deflector. Cameron White and Kevin Pietersen brutalise the ball with raw aggression, whilst Rahul Dravid and Sachin Tendulkar caress the ball with sweet timing and deft placement. Since every player has to bat, a category of batters who might be best be described as *agricultural* or *survivors* usually occupy the tail end of the innings. Their role is either to stoutly defend in support of a more-recognised batter or to swing the bat with abandon, scoring as many runs as they can in their short batting time.

Given the previously mentioned range of possible roles and styles of batting, it is little wonder that batting challenges the mind like few other sporting skills can. It provides a unique range of involvement that allows the batter to experience extreme emotional highs and lows. In most bat-and-ball sports, even after a poor performance, players have a chance to redeem themselves immediately. A baseball player strikes out and waits for eight other batters to perform before getting another chance. A tennis player loses 6-0 and serves 20 double faults but then gets to start afresh in the second set. In contrast, a cricket batter might only get to face one delivery before being dismissed from batting for the rest of the day.

However, little doubt exists that batting highs are memorable experiences. There are few better feelings in sport than making a big score under pressure. You have experienced the satisfaction of mastering an attack with immense concentration and have more than likely felt the wonderful joy that ripples through your body when a scorching drive off the sweet spot of the bat pierces the field and races to the boundary. Batters of all levels can recall such experiences vividly even when their careers are long over. Simply put, batting can be great or miserable! We hope this section gives you more chances to achieve batting highs.

Certain aspects of batting are considered essential. Sound technique enables the bat to meet the ball in the most efficient manner; good balance and footwork help you assume the correct position for playing an array of shots, and concise decision making ensures that the correct shot is played to the ball being bowled. These essentials have been previously covered in a structured manner through many of books and DVDs. This book deliberately avoids the basics. Instead, we highlight the areas of batting that are commonly forgotten or are simply misunderstood.

In this section, the art of batting is taken to another level as we uncover the secrets of being successful. It tells how one of the best one-day players of all time used the wind to his advantage. It provides a method for playing spin bowling, outlines guidance for running between wickets, and uncovers the danger signs for batters in the search for batting excellence; plus there are additional tips on preparing and starting innings, choosing placement, and creating innovative strategies. Making runs is the aim of all batters. By following the 20 points in this chapter, you just might be on the way to improving your own score.

Starting an Innings

Although every batter in the world is most susceptible at the start of innings, we rarely practice for it. Sir Don Bradman was a master at scoring a single from the first ball he faced. He was keen to get his innings underway.

Sachin Tendulkar and Jacques Kallis are also very good at starting their innings. They are both quick to pounce on anything overpitched or short, but are very watchful with anything just outside off stump. In fact, the ability to leave the ball pitched in the corridor of uncertainty (just outside off stump on a good length) is a skill in itself that should be practised whenever possible.

Another worthwhile strategy for the start of an innings is to play within the V. Play with a relatively straight bat and avoid shots that are square of the wicket. As a general rule, you should always be ready to score runs, whether you are facing the first ball or the 100th ball. The only difference is the mindset you take to the crease. If you are nervous, frightened of failing, or wayward in your thoughts, then you are not ready to start your innings. On the other hand, if you are comfortable with your preparation, confident in your ability, and mentally focused, then you are in the right frame of mind to begin.

Often it is best to maintain one key thought as you stride to the wicket. This thought varies from player to player. Some prefer to be conscious of getting right behind the ball, whilst others will remind themselves to get their feet moving. The key is finding the mental cue that suits you. This comes from training and playing as often as you can.

Consider a good putter in golf, who stands over the ball, analyses the line, and backs himself to make the putt. When you start your innings, back yourself to play the right shot at the right time. You just might surprise yourself with a very positive start and a long innings.

Seeing Off the New Ball

Former Indian star Sunil Gavaskar maintained that the first hour of a Test match was the bowler's time, and the rest of the match was his. He worked very hard to maintain his wicket against the moving ball so that he could reap the rewards as his innings unfolded.

Of course, such a tactic is more suited to longer forms of the game. In essence, the opener's role is to ensure that the bowler's advantage (the new ball) is negated sufficiently in order to set up the innings for the remainder of the team. Naturally, it is hoped that the openers set up their own innings as well.

In one-day or Twenty20 cricket, there is little time to worry about the new ball. An opener's role in these games is not only to dent the effectiveness of the moving ball, but also to ensure the run rate is maintained from the start.

All top-order batsmen must be able to turn the strike over with quick singles or to hit to the available outfield space (the option in the first 10 overs of a limited-overs game). When done well, these measures ensure more victories than losses.

Sunil Gavaskar								
	Matches	Inns	Runs	HS	BT Ave	100s	50s	Catches
Tests	125	214	10122	236	51.12	34	45	108
ODIs	108	102	3092	103	35.13	1	27	22
First-Class	348	563	25834	340	51.46	81	105	293

3

Running Aggressively

Dean Jones, arguably one of Australia's finest one-day players, was an outstanding runner between the wickets. He was not only fast, but also prepared to take extra runs at every opportunity. He would challenge fielders by being aggressive in his turn. If the fielder made a slight blunder, he was off for another run. Paul Collingwood and A.B. de Villiers are two others who consistently run aggressively.

When running between wickets, you must know where the ball and fielders are just before you begin your turn. While taking a quick glimpse, make an objective decision as to the possibility of another run. Watch your bat slide across the crease as you turn, then explode from the crease, ready to run.

Note two important points. First, when turning, position your body to face the ball; don't look over your shoulder. Second, position yourself low in the turn so you can push off with your braced foot.

When multiple runs are obvious, you may make your first turn with the bat in your preferred hand rather than facing the ball, particularly if this helps facilitate a faster turn.

Of course, you don't have to run, and you wouldn't if the ball is fielded cleanly and is on its return. However, the aim of your aggression is to pressure the fielder into a mistake and to allow you that extra run.

Dean Jones								
	Matches	Inns	NO	Runs	HS	BT Ave	100s	Catches
Tests	52	89	11	3631	216	46.55	11	34
ODIs	164	161	25	6068	145	44.61	7	54
First-Class	245	415	45	19188	324	51.85	55	185
List A	285	276	43	10936	145	46.93	19	115

4

Some Rules for Running Between Wickets

Although sensible, aggressive running is vital in an overall offensive plan, it requires two-way verbal and physical communication. Generally on first runs, the striker should call and the non-striker, who is in the more advantageous position of backing up, should react instinctively. The non-striker should assert control in the following situations:

- The striker loses sight of the ball (the ball hits the pad and bounces away at an unusual angle).
- The striker does not call immediately.
- There is any hesitation.
- The non-striker is clearly in a better position to assess the run and is running to the danger end (such as when a ball is fumbled by a keeper).

Effective running essentially revolves around good judgement, clear and concise calling, running speed, and turning speed. Efficient running (making the most of every opportunity) combines the preceding qualities with faith and trust, which evolve from training, match conditioning, and familiarity with each team-mate's style of play. Of course, if there is any hesitation, shout "No" and keep an eye on your partner. Simply turning your back is not an option.

The strike should be changed as often as possible in order to keep the scoreboard ticking over, to unsettle the bowlers, and to give each batter a minor break from ball-to-ball concentration.

Running between wickets is not an exact science because it involves human judgement. However, it is trainable and very important.

Hitting to the Gaps

How often do you see a technically efficient batter striking the ball hard to the fielders, but then failing to score? It happens at all levels of cricket. Conversely, you may be amazed when another batter, who has limited shot-making ability, seems to amass consistently good scores. In such instances, the difference between the proficient shot maker and the good scorer is the ability to hit the gaps.

When batting, it is very important to learn the art of striking the ball between the fielders. The shot doesn't always have to be forceful, as long as it is well placed. It should also allow for comfortable singles or twos to be taken. Execute a deft glance by angling the bat in the direction you wish the ball to go or by using soft hands to drop a ball into a vacant area close to the pitch. These two methods will help you score without a big shot.

You will be amazed at how easy it is to keep the score ticking over by employing this strategy. You will be even more surprised when your own score starts mounting up. After all, batting is about scoring, not just playing nice shots to the fielders!

Next time you are in the nets, imagine where the fielders might be and play to the gaps. This improves your skills in a way that is realistic to the game situation. Remember that playing the ball along the ground greatly reduces your chances of dismissal.

Jaques Kallis								
	Matches	Inns	Runs	HS	BT Ave	100s	50s	Catches
Tests	140	237	11126	189	55.07	35	53	159
ODIs	303	289	10838	139	45.72	17	78	115
First-Class	230	377	17478	200	53.77	52	91	221
Twenty20	65	65	1920	89	34.28	0	17	24

6

Dancing With the Spinners

The art of using your feet to the spinners is one of the great skills of batting that seems to have lost favour with many coaches over the last few years. Let's face it, if you can get to the pitch of the ball, you will negate spin, a key weapon of every spinner!

The confidence to come down the wicket to a spinner not only puts pressure on the bowler, but also opens up a variety of scoring options on both sides of the wicket.

It's not recommended that you dance down the wicket on every ball because that habit would play into the bowler's hand. However, if your mind is programmed to think forward, use your own judgement about whether or not to advance once the ball leaves the spinner's hand.

In fact, playing back is also part of the dance. Although you press forward slightly as you look to go down the wicket, you might actually use quick feet to get back, based on your judgement of the flight of the ball. Such footwork can affect a bowler's length, creating the loose ball you are seeking.

In recent times, Brian Lara and Michael Clarke have illustrated the value of dancing feet. They not only dance down the wicket to flighted deliveries, but also use the crease to play offensively off the back foot. Quick and decisive footwork is a nightmare for spin bowlers that often awards the initiative to the batting team.

Learn to read the spin as it leaves a bowler's hand. This allows some assurance as to where the ball is turning as you play it. The best players of spin tend to watch the bowler's wrist and finger action as the ball is released. They use these cues to predict the intended spin. For instance, when a leg-break bowler turns the wrist at delivery so that the back of his hand faces the batter, or when the ball is bowled from the back of the hand itself, it will likely be a wrong'un or a top spinner. Alternatively, some batters pick the spin in the air as it is directed towards them and play their shot accordingly.

Dance to spin and reap the rewards.

Backing Up—It's So Easy

Backing up is possibly the easiest part of cricket. You don't have any pressure from the bowler or the fielders, and you don't need to be the best batter. However, plenty of examples of neglecting this aspect of the game still exist at the highest level.

The rule states that a non-striker cannot be run out once the bowler enters the delivery stride. Therefore, all non-strikers should watch the bowler during delivery and leave the crease as he plants his back foot, just prior to release. They should also increase their momentum so that they are ready to run, assuming a position approximately 2 metres down the pitch when the bat impacts the ball.

If the ball is pitched short, a non-striker can actually get farther down the pitch without fearing that the ball will be struck straight back to the bowler. However, if the ball is pitched up, it might be struck straight down the wicket. Therefore, exercise more caution with the distance used when leaving the crease.

Whatever the situation, you must not be stationary on the batter's call. Be ready to run, have some momentum, and be alert to both the batter's call and your own assessment of the play.

Sachin Tendulkar								
	Matches	Inns	Runs	HS	BT Ave	100s	50s	Catches
Tests	169	276	13837	248	56.02	48	56	106
ODIs	442	431	17598	200	45.12	46	93	134
First-Class	272	428	22730	248	59.34	75	102	174
List A	529	516	21150	200	45.87	57	111	169
Twenty20	41	41	1437	89	39.91	0	11	18

8

Improvising— A Risky Business

Sometimes in a game, a batter has to take the initiative from the bowler. This can be a daunting task, particularly if you haven't scored for a while and the fielders are placed in very defensive positions. It is therefore crucial that you develop a slightly unorthodox way of scoring. Many of these shots have now come to the fore since the advent of Twenty20 cricket.

Some players improvise with a lofted shot, while others advance down the wicket (even to a quick bowler), looking either to score square of the wicket or to hit as straight as possible, depending on the field placements. Another option is to give yourself room by backing away slightly towards the one side. This allows you to drive a ball square on the stumps. Another improvisational method is to walk across your stumps to play to a vacant spot on the leg side. Whatever your style, watch the ball closely and maintain balance at contact.

One of the more fashionable methods, particularly late in a one-day game when the bowlers are trying to bowl yorkers, is to position yourself across the stumps and lap the ball to fine leg. You must practice this shot thoroughly before executing it in a match. Sachin Tendulkar plays this shot with aplomb.

Similarly, a reverse sweep is a risky shot. However, if perfected, it can be a surprise weapon when the outfield behind the wicket on the off side is vacant.

Switch hitting to heave the ball over midwicket has also evolved. Kevin Pietersen has perfected this art. Some play this shot with a normal right hander's grip, but Pietersen changes the position of his hands to great effect. His left-handed approach often sends the ball sailing over the boundary, much to the chagrin of the cover fielders.

If you decide to improvise, remember the risks. You must be very confident in your ability. Also, you can reduce the risk by keeping the ball on the ground. At least you won't be caught!

Reading the Game

Interestingly, most of us seem to be better players off the field than on it! We see all the mistakes, criticise the performance, and offer wonderful insights on how something should be done. That is, we say a lot until we have to actually do it.

Batting is one of the most difficult skills in cricket, simply because you often only get one chance. You must balance risk with surety, knowing when to up the attack, when to defend stoutly, and when to improvise.

In general, the best time to sum up the state of the game is at the end of each over. Learn the situation of the game by discussing strategy and exchanging words of advice with your batting partner. Likewise, when there is time to assess a game situation during a break in play, it is often useful for a coach or captain to re-emphasise the state of play.

Reading a game incorporates the following abilities:

- Summing up game situations (Is the run rate appropriate to the situation?)
- Analysing and implementing methods to support the best strategy (supporting a partner who is scoring freely)
- Adapting to the changing fortunes of a game (reducing risk when wickets are falling around you and planning to up the rate when a partnership is established)
- Assessing the opposition bowlers' strengths and weaknesses in order to negate or manipulate them (It is also useful to know which bowlers are more easily attacked.)

Although star batters are not necessarily the best readers of books in the world, they are the usually the best readers of a game.

10

Farming the Strike

The ability to turn over the strike is a very important part of batting. Similarly, sometimes it is just as important to farm the strike, maintaining it so that your partner is not exposed to a particular bowler.

An obvious instance is when a recognised batter is batting with the number 11, and more runs must be scored without concerns of time or overs. In this case, the recognised batter should work diligently to keep the strike, neglecting singles until late in an over and protecting the number 11 from facing many balls.

If, during a one-day game, a batter is left with just one or two wickets and runs are of high priority, he should work diligently to score twos or boundaries, looking for a single (or a three) late in an over.

Of course, sometimes the non-recognised batter's sole responsibility is to simply support the batter, negating the bowling rather than producing runs. Former Australian captain Steve Waugh seldom farmed the strike, since he believed every player in the team was capable of supporting him and adding to the team total.

Whatever the case in your particular team, both batters must clearly understand their responsibilities and have faith in each other to do the job.

Steve Waugh								
	Matches	Inns	Runs	HS	BT Ave	100s	50s	Catches
Tests	168	260	10927	200	51.06	32	50	112
ODIs	325	288	7569	120	32.9	3	45	111
First-Class	356	551	24052	216	51.94	79	97	273

Lofting With the Wind

H itting in the air may be dangerous, but the risk of hitting into the wind is twice that. Many times exist in a game (particularly in a one-day or a Twenty20 match) in which a lofted shot is a reasonable option. These include the end of an innings when boundaries are required to lift the scoring rate or a situation in which the fielders are surrounding the wicket area and the best option is to go over the top. When a large open space is left in the outfield, a lofted shot to that area is relatively safe.

Whatever the situation, you should always sum up the wind factor. When possible, ensure that your lofted shots are played with the wind. It is amazing how much farther the ball will go with the wind's assistance. Conversely, a ball hit into the wind tends to suspend its flight, giving fielders time to turn, run, and catch it before it lands.

Former international player Dean Jones was fastidious with his lofted shots, hoping to tail his loft on side shots (a bit like a draw shot in golf) when the wind was blowing in the right direction. His ability to implement this strategy was developed through many years of practice and refinement. Don't expect the same results without due diligence to your own training methods.

In more recent times, with the introduction of power plays and Twenty20 cricket, the lofted shot has become a major part of the game. Players like Brendon McCullum, M.S. Dhoni, Albie Morkel, and Kevin Pietersen rarely make errors with this shot. They sum up the field, target certain bowlers, and assess which end has the most helpful wind conditions.

Of course, there are times when hitting into the wind might be the only worthwhile option. Hopefully, you'll do this when the boundary is short, the outfield is empty, and there are plenty of batters still to come.

Staying Alert as a Night Watchman: Don't Go to Sleep!

Beginning an innings at the end of a day's play is often a batter's worst nightmare. We can all visualise the scene: There are 20 minutes to stumps, a wicket falls, and you have to see out the day's play. As a recognised batter, you don't have enough time to really start your innings, and you just wish the captain had used a night watchman. What if you are the night watchman? What are your responsibilities? How do you prepare? What tactics do you employ?

Of course, the answer to these questions can vary according to the conditions, the state of play, and individual batting characteristics. However, every night watchman should adhere to some basic expectations.

First, a night watchman must want to bat. Going out to bat with a defeated attitude is a recipe for disaster. You must approach the task with enthusiasm, courage, and confidence, seeing the situation as an opportunity rather than a burden.

Second, being a night watchman often elevates a batter up the order, giving him a chance to make a score the next day if he can survive those last few overs at the end of a day.

Third, the night watchman must know the best method of defence and use attacking strokes carefully. This doesn't mean that you close up and fail to look for scoring opportunities. Since the field is often up around the bat, there are plenty of gaps in which to score. Take runs when you can, putting pressure back on the fielding team. A sound defence, coupled with controlled stroke making, is always the preferred option.

Whether the established batter or the night watchman should seek more of the strike is often debated. Our preference in most instances is for the better player to take responsibility, since he has the better technique and temperament to survive.

Using the Bowling Machine Wisely

I n the last 10 years, the bowling machine has become a necessity, rather than a luxury, for the serious trainer. It has relieved the bowler from overtraining and has enabled all players to get plenty of bat-on-ball practice to improve their technical skills, particularly in problem areas.

For instance, players can set the machine for short-pitched balls in order to practice their back-foot work. Conversely, if a player is struggling with drives, the machine can provide repetitive deliveries in a designated area. Hitting more than 100 balls in just 30 minutes certainly assists skill development, as long as the skill is being practised correctly. This method of learning is often called *blocked practice*.

The machine can also be used to subtly change speed, length, or direction so that the batter learns to respond to varied deliveries. This type of random practice more realistically simulates the way that bowlers try to deceive the batter.

Once batters become accustomed to a bowling machine, they may want to seek other challenges. For instance, if the machine is set to pitch the ball on a good length, batters may use their feet to make the ball fuller. They can also try to work the ball for runs, which might be required in the latter stages of a one-day game, or hit it into a designated gap in the field. They may specifically use it to practice more unorthodox shots, such as the lap shot to fine leg or the reverse sweep.

These types of drills develop batters' capabilities, helping them extend their talents beyond the normal defensive shot to a well-pitched delivery.

Be warned that the best players use vital cues, such as body position, arm angle, and ball release from bowling actions, to initiate their shots. Use the bowling machine wisely, since nothing can replace the real bowler.

14

The Communication Triangle When an Injured Batter Isn't Running

Although it might not happen a lot, you may be asked to run for an injured batter. You will need to adjust many of your calling principles, particularly when you are standing at square leg.

First, you must present yourself at the wicket in protective gear that is identical to that of the injured batter.

Second, when the injured batter is facing, you must stay behind an imaginary, extended popping crease (usually in a square-leg position) until the ball is played. If you fail to do so, you can be run out or stumped at any time.

Third, you must run a little more conservatively, only responding and calling when definite runs are to be taken. Since three callers may be involved, remember the old saying that 'too many cooks spoil the broth.'

As a general rule, the batter should continue to call the majority of runs. Both the runner and the non-striker should respond accordingly. Of course, the non-striker can still take responsibility when a call is late or when the ball is deflected off the pads or goes behind the wicketkeeper. In all instances, the calls must be given loudly and often.

The two runners must call during multiple runs, since they may be as far as 20 metres apart. The injured runner should be aware of the situation, assisting with a call if necessary.

Running for an injured batter, particularly when he is on strike, involves the utmost concentration. Since this skill is not practised, you must rely on your own assumptions, awareness, and a very clear communication triangle.

Breaks in Batting Equal Breaks in Concentration— Be Warned!

I f we accept that starting an innings is the toughest part of batting, then we must also acknowledge that restarting an innings after a break is one of the most vulnerable times for any batter. At this stage, the batter is often comfortable—the innings is starting to bloom, some momentum is building in a partnership, and the bowlers might be starting to lose their edge. Batters beware!

The most noted mistake is the loss of a wicket directly after a drink break. During this over, all batters need to be diligent in their concentration.

Before a drink break, if a batter has been in for awhile, he is usually well settled, very focused, and, if runs are flowing, in a batting zone. He is ready and able to pounce on anything loose and to punish it accordingly, but he is also able to maintain a sound defence. After a break in play, his concentration may be relaxed, with dire consequences. When you restart your innings, flick the switch. Practise mental imagery at the end of the break to prepare yourself for play.

Batters must always resume an innings as if they are starting it again, with the utmost diligence and concentration. There is no room for complacency. If the little man in your head starts saying things like, 'I'm settled now, this is easy,' watch out! The break in play might bring a break in concentration.

Brian Lara								
	Matches	Inns	Runs	HS	BT Ave	100s	50s	Catches
Tests	131	232	11953	400	52.88	34	48	164
ODIs	299	289	10405	169	40.48	19	63	120
First-Class	261	440	22156	501	51.88	65	88	320

16

Ones and Twos Make Sense

For most centuries made, at least half the scoring shots are ones and twos, not threes, fours, and sixes. Therefore, unless you are practising for a Twenty20 game, work on controlled shots to gaps rather than big shots over the top.

Scoring singles can be the easiest part of batting, as long as you are always ready to run. Just as a deft deflection to fine leg or third man can be productive, a perfectly played, block-and-run defensive shot can produce a run. This art of turning over the strike is as important as making any boundary shot, simply because it happens a lot more frequently than the big cover drive does. Therefore, spend more time on the finer skills of your batting than on practising boundaries.

In the nets, imagine that every shot you play is a scoring shot. Make a call each time you strike the ball, even if you have blocked it down the wicket. Get in the habit so that you are ready for the quick run when the ball finds the gap or when it is hit into the infield slowly enough that a fielder would have no chance to run you out.

In recent times in one-day cricket, scoring twos when the fielders are closer to the boundary has become more of a focus. A slowly struck ball often means that outfielders must cover 30 metres or more before reaching the ball, enabling a two to be run quite safely. Balls hit wide of fine leg and third man also create opportunities for twos to be taken.

Consistent ones and twos will both improve your ability to make runs and make your batting more enjoyable. The ability to score from a defensive prod is very annoying to a bowler, but is very productive for your team. In essence, don't give away your big shots, but understand the importance of the clever ones.

Beware the Full Toss

*A*s a rather erratic part-time spinner, I learnt at an early age never to underestimate the power of the full toss as an attacking part of my repertoire. Early in my career, my teammates would often emit a loud shrill as the fullie floated down towards the wide-eyed batter. Often they would cover up all delicate body parts, turn their backs on the contest, and rarely make eye contact with me as they shook their head in disdain at my ineptness. As I got older, I still seemed to bowl high, full tosses, but I was able to camouflage them as part of my strategy because so often they had brought success.

(Ken Davis)

It is very difficult not to hit the high, full toss in the air. Batters typically try to belt the cover off the ball, only to see it lob into the waiting hands of a fielder in the deep. The secret to playing this delivery is to recognise the inherent dangers as it approaches. Hit down on the ball, but do not use full power. Place it in a gap and aim for a boundary, not a six. You can score off the ball, but make sure you see the caution light as it spirals towards your bat!

Brendon McCullum							
	Matches	Inns	Runs	HS	BT Ave	100s	50s	Catches
Tests	52	87	2862	185	34.9	5	16	162
ODIs	171	145	3569	166	29.01	2	17	189
T20Is	40	40	1100	116	33.33	1	6	125
First-Class	95	163	5339	185	34.66	9	30	267
Twenty20	98	97	2695	158	32.08	3	14	48

18

A Wicket Falls—You're In!

Often, as you wait with your pads on for a wicket to fall while chatting to team-mates about all sorts of unrelated matters, you can be lulled into a very relaxed state. Although such engagement can lighten any tension you may be feeling, it makes it difficult to perform when a wicket eventually falls. In essence, you have two minutes to get yourself physically and mentally ready to face your first delivery against a bowler, who is on top of the world at that moment.

Just as golfers and tennis players have pre-shot routines, batters in cricket must develop routines to ensure they do not drift into the contest with inappropriate focus. These are the recommended steps to follow:

- The moment the wicket falls, take a deep breath and loosen up your shoulders to relax a little.
- Stay seated and imagine the way you want to start your innings. If facing pace bowling, you might see yourself playing with a short backlift, presenting a full face, and leaving a ball that doesn't need to be played. Imagine moving your feet quickly.
- Stand up and do some running on the spot to rid your body of any lethargy.
- Walk out to bat with positive energy and practise some shots.
- Take your guard from the umpire with an authoritative tone in your voice: 'Two centres please, umpire.'
- Be quick to assert yourself on the game with strong and decisive calls. You will soon be in a flow state and on your way to another ton.

In essence, walking to the crease is a lonely exercise, full of nervous anticipation. Those who are ready to bat, both mentally and physically, are a step ahead of the rest.

Wag the Tail

Australia's success in world cricket during the late 1990s and early 2000s indicates the value of tail-end players who bat with determination, defiance, belief, and even skill. During this period, Australia recovered from a precarious position many times to control the game through the efforts of players, such as Shane Warne, Brett Lee, Glenn McGrath, and Jason Gillespie.

Opposition bowlers have difficulty countering two styles of tail-end batting. The first is epitomised by Warne, who, it has to be said, was more than a typical tail-ender. His boldness and unorthodoxy often resulted in quick runs and eased the pressure on the batter in the partnership who was more experienced. Whilst Warne was scoring freely, his partner was able to work the ball around with minimum risk.

The standard approach is to develop a rock-solid defence and the ability to work the ball for the paramount objective. You must know how to use your pads to defend balls outside the danger zone, and you should not play at balls that are not on the stumps. Most importantly, you must be a good runner. Back up and remain alert to the situation in the over to facilitate the better batter receiving more of the strike. Gillespie typified this style, impressing with his ability to play late and to move his feet both forwards and backwards when required.

We teach tail-enders to defend first and to develop shots once they have improved their technique. Since a tail-ender invariably partners a better batter, a safe, resolute, Gillespie-like approach is the most reliable way of thwarting opposition bowlers. The Englishman Ashley Giles also typified this approach.

If you are a bowler, make it your goal to win games through your batting. In a season of cricket, you can rest assured that tail-enders will have many of these opportunities, so wag your tail and become a hero.

20

Staying in by Getting to the Other End

*P*ressure builds on a batter as more dot balls are delivered. He hits the ball repeatedly to the fielders, or is unable to make adequate contact with the ball. A quick glance at the scoreboard shows that the score is stagnating, time is dwindling, and the target is getting out of reach. Look out, a wild shot is coming!

(Ken Davis)

We suspect that the preceding scenario is seen in most cricket games. We all know that the way to relieve scoreboard pressure is to create singles, but do we know how to execute that plan?

The first strategy is to look for the spaces in the field. Don't look where the fielders are; look at the gaps. With every forceful stroke, intend to hit the ball through the gaps by subtly changing the bat angle at contact. It can be bemusing when players instinctively play a shot to the delivery without any apparent quest to score. If it goes to a fielder, they say 'Well, that was the shot the ball demanded. Nice shot that, timed it beautifully. Well bowled, old chap.' Still, the player didn't score! Try something different next time. Use your wrists to direct the ball to space so you can get to the other end for a breather.

The second strategy in our search for singles is to look for tip-and-run opportunities by using soft hands at impact with the ball. Make sure your partner is backing up, let the ball come to you, and give a little at impact. Drop the ball into an area that is close to the bat but not in line with any fielder, including the bowler, and then run like the wind! For extra insurance, try to position yourself between the likely thrower and the wicket to which you are running.

The third strategy is to hit the ball to the side of the pitch with fewer fielders. Although this is typically the leg side, it may vary. If you practice turning the ball on the leg side to balls pitching on line with the stumps, you will significantly increase your capacity to score singles.

The fourth strategy is to consider the dab through the slips area if the field is not too attacking. This shot is not recommended on a bouncy, fast wicket. If the shot is considered relatively safe, let the ball come to you. Play off the back foot and use the pace of the ball to guide it through the slips area. Close watching of the ball is paramount and soft hands are an advantage.

The fifth strategy is to dance down the wicket to medium-pace bowlers or spinners and to hit wide of mid-on or mid-off. Since the momentum gained from the shot decreases the running distance compared to playing from the crease, you can often reach your ground quite safely.

Once you are locked into finding solutions with singles, you will always be up at the other end. A century is on the way.

Kevin Pietersen								
	Matches	Inns	Runs	HS	BT Ave	100s	50s	Catches
Tests	66	117	5306	226	47.8	16	20	39
ODIs	104	94	3332	116	42.17	7	20	32
T20Is	28	28	911	79	37.95	0	5	10
First-Class	153	255	11686	254	49.3	38	49	119
Twenty20	57	57	1636	79	32.72	0	9	19

Bowling

I n the middle of the 18th century, an innovative cricketer developed the overarm bowling action to replace the traditional underarm delivery. At that time, he could not have imagined the changes that would occur in the next 250 years of cricket bowling in countries around the world. During his last Test match when W.G. Grace sauntered in from the nursery end at Lord's Cricket Ground with his shirt flapping in the breeze around his substantial waistline, he could not have predicted how the simple movement he had perfected with unerring accuracy could evolve into the complex bowling of today.

As Test cricket began its journey in the late 19th century, the imposing figure of W.G. Grace took centre stage. Although he was revered more for his batting, Grace started out as a fast bowler of some renown. Throughout his distinguished career, as corpulence took over from athleticism, the pace of his roundarm deliveries subsided considerably.

I imagine that in his later years, he barely got out of a trot as he approached the wicket (my apologies to the Grace family for my poetic licence). He would have rolled into a side-on position rather than a launched one, his bowling arm would have been straight, and his roundarm delivery would have been steered. At 50 years of age, he would not have hurled the ball towards the batter.

If you contrast that image to the thundering aggression of D.K. Lillee or Malcolm Marshall, the scything swing of Sir Ian 'Beefy' Botham or James Anderson, and the prodigious spin of Shane Warne, you can see that bowling has evolved into an art form that is blessed with both raw aggression and subtlety.

Nowadays, we have doosras, zooters, knuckle balls, fast bouncers, slow bouncers, the inswing, the outswing, the reverse swing, arm balls, top spinners, and wrong'uns. The bowling arm can be straight or bent to 15 degrees. You can sling like Tait, mesmerize like Mendis, or bounce like Broad in the continual search to explore bowling's outer limits.

This section aims not to discuss the techniques of bowling, but to focus on becoming a smarter bowler in terms of both preparation and performance. In addition to discussing bowling plans, it speaks to looking after the ball like a favourite toy. It stresses persisting while controlling and masking subtle changes in each delivery. Finally, it shows the importance of adapting your bowling to cope with a variety of environmental conditions.

Bowling to Plans

Although the coaching staff might do the pre-game planning and the captain controls the on-field tactics, it is the bowler who initiates the play. Subsequently, when a team strategy is put into place, it is the bowler's responsibility to ensure the ball is delivered to suit the plan.

Consider the following examples:

• *Keeping a batter on strike.* A bowler might deliver a bouncer or a yorker at the end of an over to ensure the non-striker (who may be a weaker batter, or even a new batter) is kept on strike for the next over.

• *Bowling yorkers at the death.* With the field positioned fairly straight, the bowler aims at the batter's crease, hopefully forcing the batter to play only off or on drives. This is particularly effective during the last few overs of a one-day game, when the bowler must ensure that a batter cannot lift a ball over the field for a boundary.

• *Bowling a slower ball.* Changing pace is a crucial tactic, particularly in a one-day game when the batting team is on the offensive. It is employed to upset the batter's timing in full swing, hopefully creating a mistimed lofted shot. It may even deceive the batter to the extent that he completely misses the ball.

Like pitchers in baseball, the bowler is solely responsible for putting the ball into play. Therefore, he must be diligent in his execution, aware of the batter's strengths and weaknesses (when possible), and able to adjust to set plans as required.

Although the coach and captain are the architects who draw up the plan, the bowler starts the building process.

Sir Richard Hadlee								
	Matches	Inns	Balls	Runs	Wkts	BW Ave	Econ	5Wkts
Tests	86	150	21918	9611	431	22.29	2.63	36
ODIs	115	112	6182	3407	158	21.56	3.3	5

22

Shine, Don't Whine!

I t is often wrongly thought that a fast bowler is the only person responsible for shining the ball. In fact, the whole team is responsible for ensuring that one side of the ball is continually kept shiny. This intent not only allows fast bowlers to swing the ball when it is new, but also ensures that the ball is maintained in a condition that will eventually assist the phenomenon of reverse swing.

Reverse swing occurs when the two sides of the ball substantially differ in condition. One side is usually rougher and duller than the other, which is hopefully smoother and shinier. When bowled with the right velocity and the correct seam placement, the ball tends to swing in the direction of the shiny side.

The ability to bowl a reverse swing depends on the playing conditions. A dry, barren pitch tends to rough up balls quickly. If enough shine can be imparted to one side of the ball, reverse swing is definitely possible.

On the other hand, grassy conditions of play cause little ball abrasion, so a normal swing is a much better option.

Whatever the case, shine the ball whenever you get a chance. It just might provide the edge you are seeking.

Glenn McGrath								
	Matches	Inns	Balls	Runs	Wkts	BW Ave	Econ	5Wkts
Tests	124	243	29248	12186	563	21.64	2.49	29
ODIs	250	248	12970	8391	381	22.02	3.88	7
First-Class	189		41759	17414	835	20.85	2.5	42
Twenty20	19	19	432	492	20	24.5	6.83	0

Persist, Persist, Persist: A Bowler's Mantra

At the end of each season, a bowler is generally rated by his average or by the number of wickets he has taken. Whatever the case, if bowlers have done well at either, they have usually had a good year. However, bowlers' strike rates and economy rates are probably neither understood nor often considered.

For example, the great leg spinner Shane Warne holds countless records for wickets taken. He has done so with few runs scored against him. Although Warne's record has been amazing, very few people know his strike rate. (Have a guess! The answer is in the next paragraph. If you haven't looked yet, here's a clue: It is not as low as you would think!)

To be a great bowler on very good wickets and against accomplished batters, you must persistently land the ball on a good length and on a good line, with enough subtle variation to pressure the batter into a mistake. Warne has been a master at this. Although he (and others) may have expected a wicket every time he bowled, he had the ability and guise to set batters up by continually landing the ball in areas of uncertainty. He didn't claim a wicket every over. In fact, it took him approximately 10 overs to get a wicket! His strike rate was just under the 60 mark.

Also, because he was so accurate, he had a very low economy rate. This meant that the opposition always had to force the pace if they were to amass a respectable score. Since they were never given easy runs, they were always under pressure.

Two of the greatest bowlers of all time, Sir Richard Hadlee and Glenn McGrath, were Scrooge-like when giving away runs. They also only averaged a wicket every 50 balls or so.

So, the next time you have a chance to bowl, don't expect a wicket every time. Bowl your type of delivery with appropriate pace, swing, or spin. Bowl accurately and on a good length, and do so consistently. Before you know it, you will be getting more wickets than you thought possible, with a respectable economy rate.

24

Bowling Is Just Like Archery: Hit the Spot to Win Gold!

The ability to hit a bullseye with a bow and arrow is mandatory for any archer who wants to win an Olympic gold medal. Similarly, a dart thrower who can repeatedly pinpoint a triple 20 and a shooter who can hit a clay target within seconds of its release will both win many competitions. To even come close to achieving these results, athletes must train day after day, hour after hour. Can the same be said about bowling? The answer is obviously no, simply because more physical demands are placed on a bowler than on archers and dart throwers, who can repeat their skill without experiencing physical duress.

However, these more passive sports can teach us how to maintain concentration in order to record perfect scores on a consistent basis. Every top-line bowler in the world, from the time of Test cricket to the fashionable, shorter games of today, has been able to bowl the ball on the spot where he intended it to land. This ability does not develop without practice.

Whether you are an up-and-coming youngster or a trained professional, you must continually master your craft. Just as a baseball pitcher often practices by throwing at targets on a wall or to a catcher's glove position, a bowler should practice the skill of bowling without interference. This means that you should direct some of your training at targets on the pitch or to the hands of a wicketkeeper, rather than against batters. By doing this, you can perfect your accuracy without outside influences or the pressure of a batter. Obviously, your next test will be against a batter in the nets. Once you are confident, you can take your learned skill into the match.

Analyse, Don't Criticise!

Although it is very easy to blame others when something goes amiss, the better player looks at a performance with analytical eyes rather than critical ones. Statistics are useful indicators of performance; however, for the players and those closely connected to the team, the figures only tell half the story.

For instance, a bowler who bowls at the death in a one-day game may end up with some easy wickets, since the batting team take multiple risks in order to increase the scoring rate. For this reason, the economy rate would be a better indication of a bowler's performance in a one-day game than the wickets he took. Obviously, the ideal situation is a combination of wickets with a low economy rate. However, the economy rate is rarely displayed, particularly at lower levels of cricket. Therefore, many bowlers are given false rewards for their wicket haul.

In analysing a bowler's performance, look beyond the final figures in the right-hand column of the scorebook. The following questions must be asked of each bowler:

- Were the batters top- or lower-order players?
- At what stage of the game did he bowl?
- Did he bowl to a team plan (The object may have been to bowl negatively to certain players and more aggressively to others.)?
- Was he able to do specific jobs (Did he keep certain batters on or off strike at the end of an over?)?

Coaches who are evaluating a game closely may find it beneficial to subjectively rank each ball as good, OK, or poor. Often, perfectly executed balls (which would be ranked as good) are dispatched to the boundary along an edge or by a cross-batted slog over the leg side. Analysing bowlers in this way at least provides them with feedback on their execution, rather than just their effectiveness.

Those who are technically minded (and all coaches should be) can take advantage of the many software programs available that provide appropriate statistics.

26

Use the Wind to Your Advantage

On windy days, a fast bowler's first reaction is usually one of delight, especially if he is going to bowl with the wind behind him. Speed is at the forefront of his mind. Of course, someone has to bowl from the other end into the wind. That job is often given to the pace bowler, who is slower and more controlled. If this particular bowler can swing the ball, he should be licking his lips. The wind actually becomes a natural weapon that assists the swerve or swing of the ball. Of course, the ball will not swing just because of the wind. It still needs to be released with the correct seam position and the appropriate wrist action.

It is also worth noting that many of the fastest bowlers in the world bowl into the wind in the last overs of a one-day game. A sharp yorker is the most difficult ball to play, so it makes sense to use your best (and fastest) bowler when batters are having free swings.

Similarly, spin bowlers should be encouraged to bowl into the wind as much as possible. Nothing is harder to play than a perfectly delivered ball that dips in the air and spins on landing.

Some leg-spinners are adamant that the best condition is when the wind blows down the wicket from a leg-slip to a mid-off position (assuming that the batter is right-handed). In this instance, if the ball is given sufficient spin and delivered with appropriate flight, it will dip quickly as it reaches the batter. Hopefully, it is delivered with enough deception to create an error. More overspin on the ball will produce more dip.

Some bowlers prefer the wind to come from a first-slip position (assuming a right-handed batter). These *leggies* feel that such a wind produces a drifting effect that moves the ball slightly from left to right. The wind also slows the ball. This effect can produce a caught and bowled chance, since the batter plays too early. The ball drifts in and turns away from the batter, increasing the challenge of playing the right line.

Off-spinners, left-arm wrist spinners, and finger spinners can create similar results by using the wind to provide variation in the flight of the ball.

Whatever the case, spin bowlers must practice in all types of conditions to determine which wind direction suits them best. They must prepare a plan for bowling in any condition.

Practise Like Tennis Players

Tennis players typically practise their craft every day for at least a couple of hours. If you average a forehand every five seconds of a practice session, then a session of two hours yields around 1,400 forehands. It is no surprise that Roger Federer and Andy Murray hit the ball so precisely under pressure.

A typical cricketer at club level practises twice per week, with limited work in the off season. At most, that habit produces around 150 deliveries per week. It's no wonder that young spinners can't land the ball with the precision of Rafael Nadal's serve!

We recognise that pace bowlers need to be concerned about overuse injuries. However, if they learn a safe bowling technique, then perhaps they can undertake more skill practice. Spinners do not experience as much wear and tear on the body, so they may be able to practise more frequently.

At any rate, if you can't land the ball where you want, you are giving the batter a free hit. Why not save yourself the trouble and give him a batting tee so he can slam the ball to the boundary? Spinning the ball is one thing, but control is essential. It builds pressure on batters who are waiting for a loose ball to attempt a scoring shot.

Bowling is both a tactical and physical skill. Physically, it is a target sport, much like the serve in tennis. If you practise bowling to a spot on the pitch every day, your techniques will be more likely to stand up under pressure. Shane Warne, Andrew Flintoff, and Anil Kumble are magnificent examples of the value of control when building up pressure on a batter. Commit yourself to a daily practice of your craft, and you will also be able to make the big serve when needed.

Learn to Mask Your Deliveries

I t is often debated whether bowlers should worry about deceiving batters with their variation deliveries. Some argue that it doesn't matter, since the batters still have to deal with different deliveries. Surely, this is an excuse from bowlers who have very obvious change-ups. Subtle changes can mean that the batter will pick up cues later in the delivery, inhibiting the plan of attack.

Typically, spinners try to conceal their wrong'uns or doosras so that batters are deceived by the delivery. Most good players become excellent at reading the spin in the air. From a bowler's perspective, however, later detection creates more uncertainty for the batter. Players who read the spin well should be given a different look at the same style of delivery. For these players, bowl across the seam as well as along the seam.

Wrist spinners should learn to bowl big-spinning deliveries, as well as those that spin marginally, by altering the wrist position at release. Another useful strategy might be to bowl a very obvious wrong'un, followed by one that is more difficult to detect. Some spinners, such as Harbhajan Singh, spin both along the seam and across the seam. These deliveries, which are essentially the same, create different looks.

Fast bowlers should sometimes hide their grip on the ball with the non-bowling hand as they run in. This deters early detection of a change-up delivery. India's Zaheer Khan effectively utilises this strategy, often surprising batters with the swing direction he achieves. Faster bowlers should also try to approach the wicket with consistent velocity patterns, regardless of delivery type. The bouncer is often accompanied by an energetic run-up that does little to mask the delivery.

A good test is to ask experienced batters what they look for when studying variation balls and whether they can easily detect differences. Next, work on masking your technique to confuse everyone but the wicketkeeper!

29

Variety Is the Spice of Bowling Life

Opposite points of view often both have merit. In bowling, popular opinion seems to support the notion that control of a stock delivery is the lynchpin for success. Of course, bowlers should develop a consistent delivery that can land the ball on the spot. If practiced ad infinitum, these deliveries are more likely to stand up under pressure.

Having said that, some players possess the artistic talent to explore the wide variety of deliveries at their disposal. They challenge the boundaries and discover new techniques. Although these bowlers typically have less control over their deliveries because of the high degree of difficulty, they may be more potent in terms of wicket taking. Such players may take longer to control their art, but can form effective partnerships with tighter, more controlled bowling.

Recently, we have had the good fortune to work with an outstanding junior spin bowler. His physical assets, combined with artistic talent and intellect, are second to none. There is no doubt that he can do things with a cricket ball that even the great Shane Warne can't do.

It was inevitable that he would be judged harshly by the more conservative players in our fraternity when he entered adult cricket. He was criticised for bowling 'liquorice all sorts' in his ever-constant desire to confuse batters with subtle changes. He took a few beltings that affected his confidence. Although it was agreed that he needed to harness his quest for bowling thrills, he still needed encouragement to develop his craft and to keep from eliminating balls over which he had limited control. His thirst for discovery and experimentation needed to be nurtured. We also alerted him to the need for a reliable leg-break delivery. In short, we needed a balanced view on this issue.

At the international level, Muttiah Muralitharan and Nathan Bracken have built their substantial reputations on their ability to bowl variety balls. It remains to be seen which method works best. Clearly, we need bowlers with control because they won't be retained by captains if they don't have it. However, the artist needs more time. He should spend a portion of every training session playing with the ball to add variety to his repertoire. Those who possess the art are indeed rare. We should avoid developing clones who bowl with optimum control but limited variation. If bowling attacks are the cream on afternoon tea cakes, variety is the spice in the cream!

Andrew Flintoff								
	Matches	Inns	Balls	Runs	Wkts	BW Ave	Econ	5Wkts
Tests	79	137	14951	7410	226	32.78	2.97	3
ODIs	141	119	5624	4121	169	24.38	4.39	2
First-Class	183		22799	11059	350	31.59	2.91	4
List A	282		9416	6536	289	22.61	4.16	2
Twenty 20	29	25	525	609	30	20.3	6.96	0

30

Six-Packs Can Be Spun for More Fun!

The repetitive nature of skill practice often leads athletes to simply go through the motions in training sessions. When bowling, players are often not accountable for their actions because no one else knows their target. To give bowlers more purpose and motivation, try a group of deliveries bowled in a sequence of six (an over).

These limitless six-packs challenge the bowler's imagination. Essentially, the task involves developing a pattern of deliveries that can be utilised in a game to deceive the batter. The following examples have been used with young wrist spinners:

- Five stock leg breaks on an off-stump line, followed by one that is higher, slower, and wider (often effective with tail-end batters)
- Five leg breaks to a left-hander, followed by a wrong'un to entice a drive
- A sequence of three overspinning leg breaks, one big spinning leg break, one top spinner, and one overspinning leg break
- Four flat leg-spinners, one flighted leggie outside off, and a flighted top spinner
- A starter over: six balls delivered one-third of a metre outside off stump that are full length
- Four flighted leg-spinners (on or outside off stump), one top spinner that is shorter and wider outside off stump, and then a wrong'un on the same line
- Four short-of-length leg-spinners outside off stump that entice the cut shot, one short-of-length wrong'un, followed by leg break that is wider, fuller, and slower to entice catch-in covers

- Six leg breaks on the same length, starting on the leg-stump line and moving a little more to the off side with each delivery
- Five leg breaks followed by a backspinner (flipper or zooter)

The same approach could be mirrored with pace bowlers. When players practice these six-packs, their practice is more purposeful. They are learning to develop combinations of deliveries that might be usefully employed in games. Spin a web of six-packs and do more than impress the opposite sex!

Sir Garfield Sobers								
	Matches	Inns	NO	Runs	HS	BT Ave	100s	Catches
Tests	93	160	21	8032	365	57.78	26	109
First-Class	383	609	93	28314	365	54.87	86	407
	Matches	Inns	Balls	Runs	Wkts	BT Ave	Econ	5Wkts
Tests	93	159	21599	7999	235	34.03	2.22	6
First-Class	383		70789	28941	1043	27.74	2.45	36

Fielding

The old cry that 'catches win matches' is only part of the success story for today's cricket. In the modern game, batters and bowlers contribute to the overall outcome of a game. In addition, athletic ground fielding from all players has become mandatory. Of course, taking catches helps as well. It is no longer acceptable for fast bowlers to park themselves on the boundary, chatting to the fans, while making the occasional leisurely stroll in to field a ball that has been hit in their direction. We can no longer tolerate the presence of a portly batter who does little more in the field than walk from first slip to first slip at the change of overs.

It has taken a long time for cricketers to realise that the game is an athletic pursuit rather than a gentleman's pastime. If you don't hop on the athletic fielding train in the future, then you may be left at the station. Such is the intensity of 50-over and Twenty20 cricket that the goal for players is to be actively engaged for every ball: trying to save runs, making the most of run-out opportunities, and endeavouring to be in position to back up any errant throws that could potentially add to the opposition's score. Good teams apply pressure in the field by consistently stopping boundaries, making great catches, and throwing accurately to create run-out opportunities.

Today's cricketers are multi-skilled. Selectors now insist that players be good at two of the three main components of the game (batting, bowling, and fielding). They should also be competent in the third. A batter or bowler who is a poor fielder is often overlooked for a player who complements his major skill with an outstanding presence in the field. Complete cricketers need to develop all aspects of their fielding. This includes a sound throwing technique, the ability to catch a variety of high and low balls, and the speed to gather a hard-hit ball. These qualities must be practiced continually. Plenty of manuals provide coaching tips to assist your learning.

This section highlights 20 different aspects of fielding that will take all players and coaches to a higher level of efficiency. It does not talk about the basics. Rather, it delves further, addressing issues that most players don't even contemplate. Such aspects as anticipating the spin on the ball, backing up, positioning for relay throws, adopting a sliding technique, and utilising knee bend are some of the areas discussed that emphasise that fielding strategy and technique have come a long way in recent times. Once you have read through this chapter, your understanding of fielding will take on a new meaning. You will be on your way to becoming a complete cricketer.

Anticipating the Shot

L ike the best batsmen in the world, the best fielders seem to have time on their side. We often think that this is an innate quality. However, if you watch good fielders, you will notice that they often move to the correct position as a shot is played. They anticipate how a batsman will play a particular ball.

For instance, if you are fielding in a point position and watching the trajectory of the ball in flight, you have two options. You can brace yourself for a forceful back-foot shot if the ball is short. You can move forward into an attacking position if the ball is pitched up, given that the batsman will either defend or drive the ball forward. This is most relevant when a spin bowler is in action, since it can prevent the batsman from stealing runs from defended prods toward the point area. Jonty Rhodes, the former South African player, was a master at this. Today, the likes of Michael Clarke and Paul Collingwood will pounce on anything within their reach.

Also, if you know that a particular ball is being bowled, you can anticipate the possible outcomes. Imagine that you are fielding at mid-off or mid-on. A slower ball is being bowled. You shouldn't rush forward, since the batsman might loft the ball to your position if he is deceived during the ball's flight.

Reading the game and knowing the way that certain players bat are also key elements in anticipating outcomes. For instance, if a batter is well known for stealing short singles, you may want to field a little closer. Conversely, a batter who is obviously a slow runner can be given a little more latitude. Whatever the situation, stay alert and anticipate accordingly.

Bill Lawry								
	Matches	Inns	NO	Runs	HS	BT Ave	100s	Catches
Tests	67	123	12	5234	210	47.15	13	30
First-Class	249	417	49	18734	266	50.9	50	122

Running in Pairs

When a ball is hit into the outfield, it is most desirable to have two fielders chasing it, particularly if the chase looks likely to be close to the boundary. In such instances, the fielder who reaches the ball first will either dive or slide to stop it from reaching the boundary. If appropriately placed, he may flick the ball back to the second fielder. The second fielder should be in the stronger position to throw the ball, simply because he is not sprawled on the ground.

Also, fielders often run sideways and backwards to stop the ball. Another fielder coming from an opposite direction towards the pitch can take a flick pass in order to have forward momentum for the throw.

In some cases, the second fielder may not be required. This is based on the judgment of the first fielder to the ball, and it is regarded as an unrewarded running scenario since the second fielder has no direct effect on the play. However, running in pairs is vital for team spirit and defensive strategy. Therefore, it should be an expectation, rather than a possibility. A second fielder should always be ready to be involved.

Sir Ian Botham									
	Matches	Inns	NO	Runs	HS	BT Ave	100s	6s	Catches
Tests	102	161	6	5200	208	33.54	14	67	120
ODIs	116	106	15	2113	79	23.21	0	44	36
First-Class	402	617	46	19399	228	33.97	38		354
	Matches	Inns	Balls	Runs	Wkts	BT Ave	5Wkts		
Tests	102	168	21815	10878	383	28.4	27		
ODIs	116	115	6271	4139	145	28.54	0		
First-Class	402		63547	31902	1172	27.22	59		

Setting Up the Relay

Relay throws are important, but they should always be based on the strength of the thrower and the length of the throw. Relay throwers should position themselves approximately one-third of the throwing distance from the target, with their hands raised to provide a focal point for the throw. They should be in line with both the thrower and the target.

The responsibility of relay throwers is to ensure that they are in a ready-to-throw position. From there, they can throw to either end of the pitch, depending on the call from the wicketkeeper or from the close-surrounding fielders.

If you are throwing to the relay position, aim to keep the throw low and sharp. Don't throw high for distance. Ideally, if the throw is on target, it should skip bounce to the intended spot unless it is taken by the relay thrower.

However, always remember that a fielder who has a strong, powerful arm should aim to reach the target directly if it is within his throwing distance. This will always be faster than the relay option.

Paul Collingwood									
	Matches	Inns	NO	Runs	HS	BT Ave	100s	6s	Catches
Tests	63	109	10	4176	206	42.18	10	24	87
ODIs	186	170	35	4908	120	36.35	5	72	103
T20Is	33	31	2	561	79	19.34	0	24	12
First-Class	188	325	26	10977	206	36.71	24	0	214
Twenty20	52	47	5	855	79	20.35	0	39	16

Back Up, Don't Muck Up!

In every run-out situation, the fielding team must have someone backing up the throw. Therefore, it is every fielder's responsibility to ensure that, if he is not in the act of fielding the ball, he is assuming an appropriate position to back up or assist at the stumps at the bowler's end.

When backing up stay at least 20 metres from the stumps, if possible, to have space and time to stop any errant throws. It is also preferable to have a second fielder behind the initial back-up fielder. This provides added security, ensuring that no extra runs are conceded from overthrows.

Also, be aware of ricochet possibilities when a throw makes contact with the stumps. Although you cannot plan exactly for the direction a ball might take, you should still be ready for the unexpected deflection. Pounce on the ball to prevent any extra runs from being taken. Therefore, there should be one player directly in line with the throw and two players strategically placed at 45-degree angles to the stumps to cover the deflected ball.

A.B. de Villiers									
	Matches	Inns	NO	Runs	HS	BT Ave	100s	6s	Catches
Tests	61	105	12	4232	217	45.5	10	25	86
ODIs	101	97	14	3616	146	43.56	7	58	63
T20Is	30	29	6	579	79	25.17	0	20	32
First-Class	85	148	17	6081	217	46.41	13		132
Twenty20	69	65	12	1574	105	29.69	1	48	62

The Value of a Knock-Down

Although all fielders endeavour to field the ball cleanly, sometimes a knock-down is just as effective. This is most evident when a batter strikes a ball with great force directly to a fielder and calls 'wait,' hoping that the ball may get through and a run can be taken. A knock-down puts hesitation into the minds of both the batter and the runner. In such an instance, it is certainly an effective method of defence.

Quite often, a knock-down can be as valuable as a clean take. It can stop a boundary and keep a batsman on strike. Above all, it sets a standard of giving nothing away in the field. Diving on a ball to affect a save and knocking it to the ground can also create hesitancy in the batter's calls, often leading to run-out possibilities.

The knock-down can also be used effectively when backing up a sharp throw at the stumps. In this situation, the runner is usually scampering for a single. He will not be in a position to take another run as long as the ball is knocked down in the backup. In essence, don't ever underestimate the value of the knock-down in curtailing runs scored by the opposition.

Andrew Symonds									
	Matches	Inns	NO	Runs	HS	BT Ave	100s	6s	Catches
Tests	26	41	5	1462	162	40.61	2	28	22
ODIs	198	161	33	5088	156	39.75	6	103	82
T20Is	14	11	4	337	85	4814	0	10	3
First-Class	227	376	33	14477	254	42.2	40		159
Twenty20	78	72	13	1980	117	33.55	2	80	37

Percentage Fielding

Q uite often, a ball is struck to a fielder and the batter cannot take either a single run or an extra run (if the ball is being hit to an outfielder). In these situations, it is appropriate to play the percentages to ensure the ball does not get through your grasp. Use a more traditional fielding set-up, positioning your body and legs to stop the ball in case of a bad bounce, which may cause the ball to spill from your hands.

In general, percentage fielding is a defensive action that is very situational. It is based on variables, such as the following:

- *Game situation.* It is late in a game and conceding just one run, as opposed to further runs if fumbled, is the best option.
- *Batter's intent.* A batter is jogging through for the single and is clearly taking only one run.
- *Ground surface.* The ground is not smooth. A clean pickup is going to be tough, and the result does not hinge on a run-out!

Overall, you should play the percentages when a run-out is simply not possible.

David Gower									
	Matches	Inns	NO	Runs	HS	BT Ave	100s	6s	Catches
Tests	117	204	18	8231	215	44.25	18	10	74
ODIs	114	111	8	3170	158	30.77	7	22	44
First-Class	448	727	70	26339	228	40.08	53		280

Taking the Stumps When Appropriate

In most instances, a fielder will only take the stumps for a run-out opportunity when an obvious mix-up with the batters exists and a safe, straight throw to a fielder at the stumps rather than a direct hit is required. Other times, a close-in fielder (such as one in a bat-pad position) can get to the stumps to assist with a run-out quicker than the wicketkeeper can. In most instances, however, it is the responsibility of the wicketkeeper or the bowler to take the stumps on attempted run-outs.

When taking the ball, provide a target that is just to the side of the stumps, rather than directly over the top. Receivers often miss balls that are thrown too close to the bails because they baulk at the possibility of being hit with a flying ball or bail. It is simpler and quicker to strike the stumps with a sideways movement rather than a downward one. Also, many errors occur at the stumps when players forget to watch the ball during a catch. The courageous player stands his ground, takes the ball first, and then removes the bails.

In recent times, another method of receiving a ball has emerged. The receiver positions his hands in front of the stumps in the path of the throw, and then catches the ball while moving his hands back toward the stumps. This necessitates earlier contact and a safe, giving motion of the hands in the desired direction of the stumps.

Whatever technique you apply, you must be courageous, taking the ball in a positive manner and making sure you catch it before breaking the stumps.

38

Be a Fielder, Not a Spectator

Fielders have a responsibility in every play in which a ball has been struck into the field. The roles include the following:

- The active fielder (the one fielding, chasing, or throwing the ball)
- The second fielder, who is part of a pair when chasing a ball to the boundary or who is simply close to the active fielder in the course of play
- The receiver at the stumps, whether that be the wicketkeeper, bowler, or another fielder (when appropriate)
- The relay thrower (when a ball is hit deep into the outfield), whose responsibility is to be positioned approximately two-thirds of the way along a direct line between the thrower and the target
- The backing-up fielders, who are generally on the opposite side of the pitch to where the ball has been played (As well as backing up an errant throw, these players can also assist the fielder by calling the end to which they think the ball should be directed to provide the best opportunity for a run-out.)
- The third fielder, who can also call the end to which the throw should be directed

Despite the fact that most fielders are only directly involved in the play for a small percentage of total fielding time, all players must be prepared to initiate movement to the appropriate position based on the situation. In football terms, this is often called *unrewarded running*. Players chase opponents to maintain pressure without actually being involved in the play.

Be prepared for the time when your unrewarded running puts you into the play. Hopefully, it creates a wicket or at least saves another run.

Stay Low, Throw Low

The best fielders in the world have a low, dynamic centre of gravity, giving them good balance. They can stay close to the ground, move quickly in any direction, pounce on a slow roller, dive in either direction, and block a forceful shot, all because they are in a low position and ready for action.

Likewise, whenever they are in the field, they throw low. This is commonly referred to as a *flat throw*. They also use sufficient speed to effect a run-out. The speed of the throw must be determined by the situation. If a direct-hit run-out is required, the throw will usually be quite hard. On the other hand, if a batter is stranded, then a firm, accurate throw to a receiver would suffice. Good fielders make that choice on the spur of the moment.

Also, be aware of your team-mates' calls. Usually, a shout of 'hit' means that the ball needs to be thrown directly at the stumps. Conversely, a call of 'keeper' or 'bowler' may well indicate a throw to be over the stumps or to the side so that the relevant receiver can catch the ball and remove the bails.

When near the boundary, good fielders also ensure that their throws are flat, even preferring to bounce throw the ball to the receiver. The days of the old lob throw are numbered, simply because of the extra time it takes for the ball to reach its target.

The next time you are practicing your fielding techniques stay low, sum up the situation, and keep the throw down.

Anil Kumble								
	Matches	Inns	Balls	Runs	Wkts	BW Ave	Econ	5Wkts
Tests	132	236	40850	18355	619	29.65	2.69	35
ODIs	271	265	14496	10312	337	30.89	4.3	2
First-Class	244		66931	29347	1136	25.83	2.63	72
Twenty20	49	49	1125	1258	54	23.29	6.7	1

40

Slip It On
and Cover Them Up

Playing cricket can be a health hazard in more ways than one. When batting, a blow to the body by a fast, rising ball can cause serious damage. A knock on the finger when fielding can also be dangerous. Tremendous stress and strain are placed on a fast bowler's back when he is in the delivery stride. Of course, all these possibilities are just part of the game. Although we hope to avoid them, we accept them if they occur.

One area of concern for all cricketers is the time spent in the sun, particularly for games played in places like Australia where the incidence of skin cancer is rising dramatically. Therefore, all players must apply sunscreen regularly during a day's play. This non-invasive precaution should be compulsory.

Similarly, you must consider using sunglasses to protect your eyes from harmful rays. In the past, sunglasses were seen as fashionable rather than smart, but times have changed. Now the wearing of sunglasses has become an acceptable, intelligent precaution.

However, the advantages of wearing sunglasses must be weighed against the possible impediment to performance. Interestingly, very few (if any) batsmen wear sunglasses, yet most fielders do. Is not the catch, which might fly to a slip fielder at considerable speeds, as important as the first ball faced in a match? Why does a player see the two as different? Wearing sunglasses is certainly advantageous for your health, but is your performance assisted or hindered?

If you do wear sunglasses, ensure that you practise in them. Players often use sunglasses during a warm-up and then discard them when they take the field. Alternatively, they use their naked eyes in the lead-up to a game, but then don sunglasses when in action. Another misuse of sunglasses can often be seen in the batting warm-up. Why on earth would a batter take throw-downs while wearing sunglasses when he has no intention of batting with them?

Although we emphasise the importance of covering your eyes, we also stress the need to be fully confident in having an artificial barrier between your eyes and the action. 'Practise as you play' is a commonly accepted mantra of all professional sportspeople. If you are going to wear sunglasses, do so at training to ensure you do not compromise your performance.

Andrew Strauss							
	Matches	Inns	Runs	HS	BT Ave	100s	Catches
Tests	77	140	5777	177	43.11	18	86
ODIs	113	112	3692	154	35.50	5	49
T20Is	4	4	73	33	18.25	0	1
First-Class	199	353	14061	177	41.84	35	175
List A	240	233	7118	163	32.50	9	82
Twenty20	28	28	519	60	18.53	0	12

41

Slide for Speed, Not for Show!

When running down a ball in the field, it has become almost fashionable to slide, pick up, and throw. There is no doubt that this modern technique, if performed correctly, is an efficient fielding method. It can make the runner hesitate, and it is fast and effective. Also, if it is just outside the 30-yard inner circle, it allows a fielder the opportunity to get into position to throw with a certain degree of ease, particularly when using the bent-knee or figure-four slide.

You must read the play when considering the slide. If it will potentially help you save a run or effect a run-out, you can slide. However, if no advantage is likely to be gained, a simple pickup might save you from possible injury and dirty clothes!

When sliding near the boundary, make sure you time your slide to stop the ball. Your main aim in this situation is to stop extra runs, not to effect a run-out. The method is less crucial, but the save might be a match winner. Go for it with confidence and purpose. Hopefully, whilst you are sprawled on the ground, another fielder will be nearby to pick up the ball and return it.

Also, be aware that sliding on hard grounds is not advisable. Although first-class players have the luxury of a soft, smooth surface, most local players have to endure hard, rough grounds. Be sensible, consider the conditions, and slide when appropriate.

Dennis Lillee							
	Matches	Balls	Runs	Wkts	BT Ave	Econ	5Wkts
Tests	70	18467	8493	355	23.92	2.75	23
ODIs	63	3593	2145	103	20.82	3.58	1
First-Class	198	44806	20695	882	23.46	2.77	50
List A	102	5678	3259	165	19.75	3.44	1

42

'Bend ze Knees!'

I can still hear the anguished cry of my ski instructor as I plummeted towards the edge of a crevasse on my first venture on the ski slopes. 'Bend ze knees,' he pleaded, as my ungainly attempt to balance those unmanageable extensions of my feet predictably ended in catastrophe.
(Ken Davis)

Bending the knees is just as important in cricket for creating quick movement and generating power from the lower body as it is in skiing. When fielding in slips, youngsters commonly adopt a stance with minimal knee bend. In order to move up or to the side, straight-legged players must bend their knees before pushing off to create the desired movement. It is far more efficient to start with a bent-knee stance so that when the ball is hit within your area, you can instantly push off in the required direction. A bent-knee stance in slips also makes it easier to catch balls that are hit low.

Straight-legged fielders tend to bend from the trunk. They are usually moving down towards the ball as contact is made. Consequently, the ball often drops out of the catcher's hands. Bending the knees provides a more stable base and produces minimal downward movement for low balls, increasing the likelihood that the hands will be in a more favourable catching position.

The same principle applies to ground fielding in the infield (as mentioned in chapter 39). If you bend your knees when walking in with the bowler, you can move more rapidly in any direction. You will also be in a better position to field a low-hit ball.

In addition, if you bend your knees in the batting stance, you should be able to move more quickly and to use your legs more effectively to generate force in your strokes.

43

Become a Star Fielder off Your Own Bowling

The exploits of top fielders, such as Ricky Ponting, A.B. de Villiers, and Andrew Symonds, are exciting to watch. They are so focused, throwing themselves at the ball with such desperation that they often create run-out and catching opportunities. Nothing hit within a body length of them can be considered safe. They want the ball to be hit to them. They are so courageous in their quest to field the ball.

Bowlers frequently allow the ball to get past them because they lack this preparation and desperation. It is almost as though they are surprised that the ball could be hit to them after they bowl. Spin bowlers should be geared for a ball coming back to them in particular, since the drive shot is often played against them. Additionally, spinners should always be alert for a caught-and-bowled possibility, since their art is all about deceiving batters with subtle variations in flight and pace.

However, it is just as important for them to field balls that are hit along the ground. A ball hit past the bowler typically produces a score, releasing pressure on the batter. If bowlers can field a ball that is hit powerfully back to them, then batters might become frustrated by the fact that their good shots are being fielded. Subsequently, they may try to force the issue, potentially creating errors.

Fast bowlers are usually very poor fielders off their own bowling. Many would argue that they don't have time to get down to the ball, since they are still following through after their delivery. Sure, it may be tough, but if you bowl a ball that is full in length and on the stumps, then you should expect it to come back to you. Get prepared!

Bowlers often become spectators after the ball is hit into the field, failing to get back to the stumps in time to receive the ball. It is a pity that they don't emulate part-time spinners like Michael Clarke and J.P. Duminy, who are full of energy. They hustle back to the stumps if the slightest chance is on offer. Frequently, spinners get their hands to the ball, but let it get through for runs. Many become a little precious about their spinning fingers, failing to go at the ball with enough commitment and strength of purpose.

After bowling the ball, you should adopt an aggressive, alert stance, with your weight balanced on your toes and your knees bent for action. You should be like a tiger, ready to pounce on its prey. Be prepared to dive for the ball and get down low so that you are like the proverbial brick wall. Make your captain proud when you field off your own bowling. You will create wickets for the team.

Muttiah Muralitharan								
	Matches	Inns	Balls	Runs	Wkts	BW Ave	Econ	5Wkts
Tests	133	230	44039	18180	800	22.72	2.47	67
ODIs	337	329	18169	11885	515	23.07	3.92	10
T20Is	11	11	258	266	13	20.46	6.18	0
First-Class	232		66933	26997	1374	19.64	2.42	119
Twenty20	66	66	1523	1569	83	18.9	6.18	0

44

Making Run-Outs Routine

With an ever-increasing focus on athletic fielding, you must specifically prepare to routinely make run-outs. With this in mind, we have designed and tested a drill that we think creates pressure and intensity similar to game situations. It also replicates match angles of attack and release.

The Infield Hustle

The infield hustle has the following scoring system that provides measurable feedback for players.

Scoring Procedure

Players receive one point for an attack on the ball, one point for handling the ball cleanly, and three points for hitting the stumps or returning the ball within easy reach of the keeper or the bowler in the second phase of the drill.

Format of Drill

- Players are divided into groups of five or six.
- For the first seven minutes, players aim to hit the stumps.
- Replicating game shots, a batter hits the ball from a feeder.
- Fielders are positioned at point, cover, mid-off, square leg, mid-wicket, and mid-on. In other words, the infield is fairly standard. Essentially, fielders go to their normal positions, but flexibility is encouraged.
- Rapid movement is key. Players should squeeze as many attempts into seven minutes as possible. Spare balls must be available.
- A scorer records individual scores for each fielding attempt.

- After 7 minutes, 15 additional attempts are made. This time, a throw-over the stumps to the keeper or bowler is made. If the ball is dropped or thrown outside the easy-reach zone, no points are awarded.
- A wicketkeeper can be recruited. A player can also act as a keeper using a baseball glove. For these last 15 attempts, there can be two or three fielders on the off side and two on the leg side, depending on whether the wicketkeeper is from the fielding side or not.

Assessment

At the end of the drill, all scores are added up and divided by the number of attempts completed in the time allotted. A reasonable target is around 60 attempts. As a rough guide at the club level, you should expect scores in excess of three to be achieved.

The value of this drill is that it is specific to the game. It can be repeated many times over as a measuring tool for infield improvement. Individual scores can also be maintained and compared, provided fielders are in the same position. The short session ensures that intensity is maintained. Coaches should make sure that fielding distances are the same so that comparisons between sessions are reliable.

Cameron White								
	Matches	Inns	NO	Runs	HS	BT Ave	100s	Catches
Tests	4	7	2	146	46	29.20	0	1
ODIs	72	59	12	1766	105	37.57	2	33
T20Is	23	22	8	513	85	36.64	0	11
First-Class	112	188	24	6873	260	41.90	16	105
List A	184	158	24	4762	126	35.53	6	82
Twenty20	84	79	21	1888	141	32.55	2	32

45

Batters Can Spin, Too!

When we watch juniors in the field, we frequently see players making errors because they cannot read how the spin on the ball causes deviations in flight and rebound. A classic example of this occurs for point fielders. The ball is often sliced towards point. However, after contact with the ground, it spins backward from point, often eluding the outstretched hands of unsuspecting fielders.

Whenever a ball is hit off centre, spin will be created. You must understand its effects and make fielding adjustments accordingly. If a ball is aimed directly from a right-handed batter to a cover fielder but is not hit in the centre of the bat, it typically curves away to the left-hand side of the fielder. If you listen to the contact, you should be able to detect a ball that is hit more with the edge of the bat than with the middle.

If a right-handed batter clips the ball off his pads behind square leg, it also tends to spin on contact with the ground, this time towards fine leg. You need to be ready for this deviation when fielding in the square-leg region. A square cut that is hit underneath the centre of the ball and high in the air creates backspin on the ball. The ball tends to curl away from a fielder who is running from point to third man to catch the ball.

Listen to the sound of the ball striking the bat and be aware of off-centre hits. Next, be aware of flight characteristics and the rebound direction of these strokes. Move to a position to account for the spin. You should never be surprised by a ball spinning from a batter's stroke.

John Buchanan								
	Matches	Inns	Runs	HS	BT Ave	100s	50s	Catches
First-Class	7	13	160	41	12.30	0	0	5
List A	1	1	64	64	64.00	0	1	1

Bounce the Ball Into the Keeper's Gloves, Not at His Shins!

n bygone years, fielders would throw balls in from the deep with trajectories that would have made pilots of low-flying aircraft anxious. The crowd would break out in spontaneous applause as the throw would, almost magnetically, nestle in the gloves of the wicketkeeper, just above the bails. Ah, such control!

Unfortunately, this approach seldom produced a run-out because the ball took too long to get to the keeper. We have since progressed to the method of throwing the ball hard and flat to our intended target in order to create possible run-outs. Often, when a run-out is on, a bounce throw may be preferred to a throw over the stumps because it gives the fielder two chances to execute a run-out. He should either hit the stumps or have the keeper catch the ball and remove the bails.

In trying to bounce the ball in or hit the stumps, players often make the ball bounce within a metre of the stumps. This makes it very difficult for the receiver (either with or without gloves) to take the ball if it misses the stumps. A close run-out requires a bounce throw that neither goes over the stumps nor bounces just in front of the receiver.

Shane Warne								
	Matches	Inns	Balls	Runs	Wkts	BW Ave	Econ	5Wkts
Tests	145	273	40705	17995	708	25.41	2.65	37
ODIs	194	191	10642	7541	293	25.73	4.25	1
First-Class	301		74830	34449	1319	26.11	2.76	69
Twenty20	45	45	984	1225	46	26.63	7.46	0

47

Use the Right Throw at the Right Time

I magine you are chasing a ball towards the boundary. You pick it up and prepare to launch it back to the wicketkeeper. What are your choices in this situation? What should be running through your head as you approach the ball?

The cricket computer inside your head should be ticking over as you chase the ball down: 'Which way is the wind blowing? Can I throw the ball hard and flat to the keeper? Will I be better served throwing to a cut-off player for a relay throw? Can I execute a flick pass to a player who is running in from the outfield? Is the ball likely to be in a position where batters may be tempted to take an extra run? To which end are my team-mates calling me to throw? Which runner is slower?'

In order to make the right choice in each fielding experience, you need to know at which distances you can throw the ball hard and flat. Golfers know exactly how far they can hit each club, so why shouldn't fielders learn which type of throw should be executed from different distances? To facilitate this process, each player should be tested from different distances in the following manner:

- A throw is made from three distances (30, 40, and 50 metres).
- The player is timed from the starting position, which is 10 metres from the stationary ball, until the ball hits the keeper's gloves.
- Three different techniques are trialled at each distance.

Here is the set-up for the 40-metre throw:

- The following techniques are to be used for each distance:
  1. Pick up the ball, brace with your right leg (for a right-handed throw), and throw as hard as you can from a balanced, set position.

2. After pickup, do a crow hop and throw hard and flat to the keeper.

3. Use a relay throw.

Just as golfers consider the wind and environmental conditions before playing their shots, you will need to factor in the force of the wind and the quality of the ground surface. For example, let's say that you determine in still conditions that you have a fastest time from 40 metres with the first technique from the preceding list (pick up and throw from a set position). If you are throwing into the wind from the same distance, you may be better served using a crow-hop technique. Similarly, if the surface is firm, you should throw hard and flat, skipping the ball to your target.

Throw choices depend on the position on the ground where the throw is to be taken and the strength of each person's arms. Because no two players are alike, your throwing capabilities need to be put to the test so that you are better equipped to make the appropriate choice during a game.

In essence, know which throwing techniques are most efficient for you at different distances and choose the appropriate method for the conditions. By doing this, you may make some run-outs that you once thought were impossible.

48

Swarm Like Bees to the Honey Pot

*S*ome time ago, I was fortunate enough to play a game against an MCC touring team captained by Mike Brearley. Now, in contrast to many of its predecessors, this English team was outstanding in the field, with notables such as David Gower and Derek Randall leading the pack.

I can remember batting that day and was engaged in two run-outs in a relatively short period of time. In the first instance, I burnt my captain by calling 'Yes' then 'No' as I felt the fielders swarming to a ball that I initially thought was an easy single. Alas, run-out number one! Not long after, my new partner called me for a run that left me sprawling on the pitch in a vain attempt to make my ground. Perhaps he decided to get in first!

(Ken Davis)

After these dismissals, the ground that the fielders made from the time the batter settled in to prepare for the ball until he hit it was apparent. Some players moved 10 metres in that time. Granted, they may have been quick, but it was this sense of swarming that created the most difficult adjustment.

When next you field, see if you can create this opportunity. (Remember that fielders may only move towards the batter once the bowler begins the run-up. They are not permitted to deviate sideways from this line.) The swarming effect may help you make some run-outs. Go for the honey pot!

Ian Chappell									
	Matches	Inns	NO	Runs	HS	BT Ave	100s	6s	Catches
Tests	75	136	10	5345	196	42.42	14	15	105
ODIs	16	16	2	673	86	48.07	0	7	5
First-Class	262	448	41	19680	209	48.35	59		312

49

Set the Table

When you have guests for dinner, you invariably take great pains to place people in specific seats with all the utensils at their fingertips so that meaningful interaction with food and people can occur. Yet when we play cricket, we invariably present players with a smorgasbord of options in the field. Granted, we are typically told where to position ourselves in the field, but we are not in a great situation to modify our positions for different deliveries.

If we know which fork is appropriate for use with a certain food, we can confidently attack its consumption. In cricket, we don't know what the bowler is going to serve up. Therefore, flexibility in field positioning is somewhat of a gamble. Wouldn't it make more sense for the fielders to know when a bouncer, yorker, or slower ball is imminent?

Set plays are prevalent in most team sports, with basketball, soccer, gridiron, and baseball perhaps leading the way. Cricket has been slow to pick up on this trend, but there are signs that this is changing. In addition to the bouncers, yorkers, and slower balls, set plays could be established for a leg-side stumping to a player who is intent on getting on the front foot or for a change in spin delivery. For example, a leg-break bowler bowling a wrong'un might produce subtle changes in fielding position.

It's time for cricket to stop serving up a buffet of possible deliveries that leave the fielders in just as much doubt as the batters are. They must know the pace, direction, and speed of the ball that is coming so that they can anticipate likely batting responses. Set the table methodically and give players an opportunity to read the signals and to select the appropriate fielding utensil.

50

Cricket Is Not Baseball

When searching for a competitive edge, many sports look for stimulating ideas outside their own domain. In cricket, baseball concepts and approaches have been borrowed to good effect. Throwing programs are commonplace in most elite squads. As a result, good throwing and fielding techniques are now expected from all first-class players.

However, in our efforts to replicate the baseball way, some have forgotten the two most glaring differences between baseball and cricket: target size and throwing angles. With respect to baseball, the target of a throw is usually much wider than in cricket. A baseball infielder who throws to first base has a margin of error based on the size of the first baseman. In fact, he could throw to the feet of the first baseman, to an extended arm raised above the first baseman's head, or even a metre or so to either side (a differential of approximately 6 square metres) in order to get an out. On the other hand, an infielder in cricket must either hit the stumps or get very close (if throwing to the wicket keeper) to effect an out. This target area is less than 1 square metre.

Furthermore, cricket players have much more variation in throwing distance. Depending on the fielding position, this can be anywhere in a 360-degree arc of the batter. As a comparison, a shortstop in baseball throws somewhere between 30 and 40 metres. In one-day cricket, with a set infield circle having a radius of 30 metres, players at cover may have to throw a maximum of 25 metres if the ball is hit straight to them, provided they move in to field the ball. Those fielding at point will have throws varying in distance from approximately 25 metres (to the wicketkeeper) to as much as 35 metres (to the bowler's end). In addition, since the distance between bases is longer than a cricket pitch (by about 7 metres), a baseball infielder may have more time to execute an out at first base.

The major point here is that cricketers in the infield, on most occasions, must throw a shorter distance than a baseball player does. Therefore, a quick release may be more efficient than preparation to throw from an optimum-power position.

In essence, although you should learn the correct techniques of throwing and should understand the basic fundamentals of body position for executing a powerful throw, you must always remember that cricketers (unlike baseball players) have to throw from different distances and angles, and in a variety of game situations. It is too simplistic to say 'take your time, get balanced, and get aligned in a power-throwing position.' Sometimes, you just need to get the run-out with the shortest and fastest throw. It may be a little ungainly, but it will hopefully be balanced.

Leadership

L eadership has been a feature throughout history in world affairs, local communities, business, families, and sport. We think of Churchill, Napoleon, Hitler, Gandhi, and Mandela as examples of political leaders who have shaped society, both positively and negatively. Business tycoons such as Rupert Murdoch and Kerry Packer have altered media throughout the world. Many people have made significant contributions to the development of athletic excellence through their unique approach to leadership. A few examples include gridiron coach Vince Lombardi, swimming guru James Counsilman, soccer manager Alex Ferguson, and tennis maestro Harry Hopman.

Traditionally, cricket teams are led entirely by a captain, both on and off the field. However, in line with most other sports, cricket has recently introduced non-playing coaches. They direct and manage the preparation of players and assist the captain with tactical issues that emerge in the game. A range of specialist coaches also commonly assist at many levels of cricket.

Essentially, the task of leading players on the field still rests with captains. They set the field, decide on bowling changes, and motivate players to elevate their performance. Captains of successful teams include both outstanding players (Sir Don Bradman, Clive Lloyd, and Richie Benaud) and those whose playing ability was not as dominant (Mike Brearley). In the latter case, his astute tactical mind enabled his team to seize critical moments in games for the win, which certainly compensated for any perceived deficiencies in his playing skills.

Although most captains have been batters, several outstanding all-round cricketers have led their teams well, such as Kapil Dev, Sir Ian Botham, Sir Garfield Sobers, and Richie Benaud. It is hard to assess, but their outstanding example on the field probably allowed them to lead so effectively. Specialist bowlers have been less likely to emerge as captains, possibly because the arduous nature of their role affects their ability to think clearly and plan ahead. It could also be, as many of us batters and all-rounders think, that bowlers (particularly fast bowlers) are from a different breed that is not smart enough to lead!

In recent times, coaches have played a more significant role in world cricket. This has filtered down to all levels of the game. John Buchanan, Andy Flower, and Mickey Arthur are just a few of the non-playing coaches who have clearly guided their squads through successful eras. They seem to have developed a good rapport with their captains and have worked together to enhance the preparation and performance of their respective teams.

This section explores the art and science of cricket leadership from the perspectives of both the captain and the coach. For the captain, it considers what happens after winning the toss, field placements, the importance of presenting a positive body image, creative planning of bowling changes, and the timing of team declarations when batting. It examines how coaches can best teach skills and what coaches and players should expect of one another. It also considers the constant challenge of providing specific preparation for cricketers.

To Bat, or Not to Bat— That Is the Question

Over the years, the general consensus has been that if you win the toss, you will elect to bat 9 times out of 10. On the 10th time, you will consider bowling, but will end up batting anyway! There is certainly merit in this thinking. First, most teams would prefer to put runs on the board than to chase a total. Second, the pitch (if it is turf) normally deteriorates with use. Third, the chance of controlling the flow of the game in non-limited over matches is greater.

Although these reasons all support the decision to bat, sometimes bowling might be the better option. Consider the following examples:

- When a game is played under ordinary conditions and a team must dismiss the opposition (or force the opposition to declare) to gain a win, the bowling team effectively has two ways of stopping an innings. One is in their own hands (claiming 10 wickets) and one is in the batting team's hands (a declaration).

- A pitch that is affected by rain clearly offers assistance to the bowlers.

- When humidity is high and cloud cover is dense, swing bowlers are at an advantage.

- New wickets and a pitch with a good cover of grass favour bowlers.

- If batting is your strength and you are prepared to chase whatever the opposition set you (given you do not get 10 wickets!), you can choose to bowl first.

Whatever your decision, be confident in your choice and ensure that your reasoning is sound and objective. Essentially, players need to adapt to any challenge in front of them.

52

Avoid Pressuring Bowlers

B owling is a precise art. Deliveries that are a little short or a little full can lead to punishment. Subsequently, allow bowlers on top to work with freedom; do not place undue pressure on them. Often, after a bowler has taken two or three quick wickets, the captain responds by adding more slips, more bat pads, and few defensive fielders.

Although this can be an important strategy for maintaining pressure on batters, sometimes opening up gaps in the field actually pressures the bowler. Think of a bowler who has success directing the ball at the stumps with slight movement away from the batter. If, for example, more slips are added and the leg-side field is left open, the bowler's tendency will be to bowl a little more outside off. He knows that any ball that is not perfectly pitched will be easily dispatched into the leg side, allowing for easy runs and possibly taking pressure off the batter.

In essence, simply placing more players in catching positions is not always the smartest move. Allowing the bowler freedom and making it difficult for a batter to score can be just as effective. Next time, before you start attacking too much, consider your bowlers and the effect a field change will have on them.

Gary Kirsten								
	Matches	Inns	Runs	HS	BT Ave	100s	50s	Catches
Tests	101	176	7289	275	45.27	21	34	83
ODIs	185	185	6798	188	40.95	13	45	61
First-Class	221	387	16670	275	48.31	46	79	171
List A	294	289	9586	188	36.58	18	58	97

Get the Angles Right

Cricket is a game made up of angles. A leg before wicket decision can be determined by the perceived angle the ball will take after hitting the pads, particularly if a batter is hit on the pads when he is not playing a shot. Similarly, the angle of the bat determines whether the ball is lofted or hit along the ground. Of course, a batter has 360 degrees in which shots can be played.

Subsequently, the captain, in consultation with the bowler, must ensure that the fielders are appropriately placed to shut down scoring options. This means that the angles must be manipulated appropriately.

Fielders should not be placed behind each other. A third man, for instance, should bisect the close-in fielders. Similarly, the shorter, wide mid-on (used invariably with leg-spinners) should be appropriately placed to cut off the straight-on drive. This leaves a wider gap square of the wicket, forcing the batter to hit across the line of the ball on the leg side.

The importance of getting the angles right in field placements should not be underestimated. When a catch is taken in an unorthodox position, don't assume it is lucky. Maybe the captain just happened to get the angle right.

M.S. Dhoni								
	Matches	Inns	Runs	HS	BT Ave	100s	50s	Catches
Tests	48	73	2602	148	40.65	4	18	127
ODIs	172	153	5733	183	50.28	7	37	170
T20Is	25	24	441	46	25.94	0	0	11
First-Class	89	139	4764	148	37.51	7	32	235
List A	228	205	7735	183	49.58	13	48	237
Twenty20	78	71	1688	73	35.16	0	7	32

54

Remember the Mid-On

Some captains and bowlers set fields without having a mid-on. They may be forgetting that a push or drive to the mid-on area is one of the easiest shots for most batters, particularly for balls that are slightly overpitched and are directed at the stumps. Good players simply move their feet across their stumps and guide the ball to the vacant mid-on position to take easy runs.

In general, bowlers aim at off stump. When bowlers slightly err with length, they don't want batters to score easily by playing a straight shot past them. At best, a mid-on denies easy runs to this area. If positioned correctly, it may entice a batter to hit across the line to a squarer position. Hopefully the ball will be missed, creating a leg before wicket chance. Although a mid-on can be considered a conservative position, do not underestimate the value of denying easy runs in order to get a wicket. Keeping a batter on strike pressures the batter to score, hopefully forcing a mistake and, ultimately, a wicket.

The only time a mid-on can be avoided is when a very fast bowler wants to bowl some short deliveries in which the ball is not pitched up, therefore denying the possibility of straight drives. However, if this is your strategy, ensure that the bowler sticks to the plan. He could also bowl a full delivery outside off stump, thus restricting the likelihood of an on drive.

Daniel Vettori								
	Matches	Inns	Balls	Runs	Wkts	BT Ave	Econ	5Wkts
Tests	100	165	24997	11007	325	33.86	2.64	18
ODIs	255	240	12111	8367	268	31.22	4.14	2
T20Is	28	28	649	580	35	16.57	5.36	0
First-Class	152		35722	15920	499	31.9	2.67	28
Twenty20	57	57	1282	1321	67	19.71	6.18	0

The Second New Ball— Overrated or Not?

In first-class cricket, captains have the option of taking a second new ball after 80 overs (The rules governing taking a second new ball may vary slightly in local competitions and in different countries). For most, the initial reaction would be to take advantage of the swing, bounce, and carry that a new ball offers. However, shrewd captains are a little more wary, weighing the advantages of this choice against the subtle disadvantages that may not be as obvious to the novice skipper.

For instance, if the game situation demands that runs be contained, and the spinners and medium pacers are doing just that, you might be better off sticking with this plan. The batters may get themselves out by trying to force runs. If the spinners are on top and creating chances in the field, you might stick to an all-spin attack. This is certainly a good option when the pitch is either taking spin or keeping low. Likewise, if the bowlers are having success with reverse swing, you would be inclined to stick with this option. A new ball, which swings conventionally, might not be as effective because its movement is generally a little easier to detect.

Captains should also take the freshness of the fast bowlers into account. If the option is to take the new ball, the quicks must be fully rested and ready to go. Of course, if the state of the game demands quick wickets, and you have explored most options, you should probably choose a new ball. Be aware that runs can come quickly, since the new ball will fly off the bat. For this reason, a third man becomes almost compulsory with the second new ball.

If you are the captain, remember that this choice requires a thorough analysis of the game situation, an understanding of the capabilities and fitness of your fast bowlers, and just a touch of luck.

56

Be Positive—
It's Infectious

It is often troubling when a captain berates a team-mate for a mistake. It could be a dropped catch, a fumble in the field, or possibly a wayward delivery from a bowler. No doubt the player would not have meant to make the mistake. The captain will surely be disappointed, since the mistake might cost a wicket or some runs, but the player is often just as upset as everyone else in the team.

Think of a young child who drops an ice cream on the floor and proceeds to cry incessantly because of the loss. Should the parent discipline the child for the mistake or console him? Like a captain, the parent has to quickly assess the reason for the situation. Was it a result of carelessness or was it simply an accident?

A captain certainly has the right to make players aware of their mistakes, particularly if he believes the players have not made every effort in their performance. However, a player who is trying his best and concentrating hard should not be ostracized. In fact, the opposite should occur. Good body language and some positive words to deflect the mistake will ensure that the player does not carry disappointment into his next action on the field.

Handling players in the field and talking to them after the game is extremely important. Your body language, speech, or written evaluation provide feedback that reflects your opinion of their performance. Although you must be honest in your analysis, you must also be tactful and respectful of both effort and performance. In general, be positive rather than negative. It can be infectious!

Place Your Fielders Strategically

Coaches are forever disappointed when a run-out opportunity is missed because the wrong fielder is in the wrong place at the wrong time. Although we expect all fielders to be competent, it would be naïve to think that every player is equally skilled when it comes to specific areas of fielding. Some players have excellent reflexes and soft hands, suiting them for a slip position. Others with rocket arms can throw accurately from the boundary. Those with agility and an ability to release the ball quickly are usually best suited for the inner circle.

When you are seeking a one-percenter (something that gives you a slight edge over your opposition), pay attention to detail when positioning fielders. For instance, the best, most agile throwers should be used square of the wicket (point or square leg). This area is typically the most difficult for batters in their calling, thus producing a mix-up and a possible run-out opportunity.

Similarly, late in a one-day game, when the batting team is pushing for extra runs from balls hit deep into the outfield, you must put your strongest throwers on the boundary. This will either stop an extra run or produce a run-out if the batters take on the fielder. You can also position quick fielders next to slower ones to achieve a balance in speed. Two slow-moving fielders next to each other can easily be exploited by alert batters.

Captains must be diligent when placing the field. If that means that certain fielders have to move between balls to assume the run-out position (as is often the case when left- and right-handed batters are at the wicket), then it must be done. Leaving players in positions for which they are not suited is both a missed opportunity and a recipe for disaster.

58

Create the Unexpected

Mark Taylor was considered one of Australia's greatest captains. He had a terrific win-loss ratio, but it was his tactical awareness and creative thinking that elevated him above many of his peers.

During a test match at the Melbourne Cricket Ground, the game was meandering along. The batsmen appeared set and the bowlers were bowling reasonably well without really threatening to take a wicket. Then, the master struck, introducing Ricky Ponting into the attack. Ponting has never been considered an all-rounder. At this stage of his career, his part-time medium pacers were usually left in the training nets. However, on this day, he was given a bowl just before a break. As silly as it sounds, he got the breakthrough wicket.

This example highlights the need for captains to think outside the square in order to create a positive outcome. You must still maintain pressure. Taylor knew that Ponting was skilled enough to do this, albeit for a limited time. There must also be some logic in your decision.

Michael Clarke, a bowler who was hitherto unknown, was introduced into the attack in India during his first Test series in 2004. He produced a stunning display, routing the innings with figures of six wickets for just nine runs and helping Australia win the Test match. This was an amazing piece of captaincy!

Another example is a simple fielding shift. This once occurred when a very experienced batter was well set and was scoring freely in front of the wicket. He was not known to play the cut shot a lot, and he very rarely glided anything to third man. In order to change the tempo of the game, the two slips were removed, leaving a wide gap between the keeper and point. A third man was put in place. Sure enough, at the first opportunity, the batter attempted a glide to third man for the easy single. Instead, he feathered an outside edge to the keeper, who duly took the catch. This positive outcome came from some creative thinking.

In the Ashes series of 2005, England captain Michael Vaughan adopted some innovative field placements that unsettled the much-vaunted Australian side. His tactic of bowling around the wicket to left-handers with a deep point was designed to dry up players, like Adam Gilchrist, who were normally free flowing. It proved to be successful. Also, a short mid-off was set to Matthew Hayden, which not only blunted his scoring, but also brought about his dismissal.

In batting, there is probably less margin for error. Batters are usually given a designated position in the order and are expected to play their role. Sure, you can occasionally throw a pinch hitter into the innings to elevate the scoring, but batting order is generally fairly rigid. However, this thinking was once ignored in 1937. Sir Don Bradman was both a gifted batsman and a shrewd skipper. On one occasion, he decided that the pitch was in such an ordinary condition that he sent in the normal number 10 and number 11 batsmen to open the innings. He said this was because 'they would have as much chance of surviving as the openers!' Of course, he was proved right. As the pitch improved and the more-accomplished, top-order batters came to the crease, they were able to bat normally. In fact, Bradman batted at 7 and made an incredible 270 to help Australia win the Test match.

Although captaincy is based on sound principles, the most exceptional captains seem to create the unexpected at just the right time.

Mark Taylor								
	Matches	Inns	NO	Runs	HS	BT Ave	100s	Catches
Tests	104	186	13	7525	334	43.49	19	157
ODIs	113	110	1	3514	105	32.23	1	56
First-Class	253	435	20	17415	334	41.96	41	350

59

Declarations Must Optimise Your Chance of Winning

I n recent times, the Australian captain Ricky Ponting has sometimes waited to declare in order to help a batter reach a milestone. The most notable example is when Brad Hodge made his maiden Test century in Perth. He was given time to complete a memorable double century before a declaration was made. Australia had more than a day to dismiss the opposition, but they narrowly failed to achieve a victory. Did Ponting err here by putting individual achievement ahead of team results? Contrast this to the following Test match in 1971. Bill Lawry declared when Rod Marsh was a few runs short of becoming the first Aussie keeper to make a 100.

When you choose your timing for declarations, you must not take any notice of individual milestones. The aim is always to optimise your chances of getting a result. You must consider the strength of the opposition batters, the condition of the wicket, and your bowlers' ability to exploit said conditions.

The safest declaration is to give the opposition no chance to make the required runs. However, you also need to be sure your bowlers can dismiss 10 batters, who are essentially intent on digging in with minimal risk. A declaration that is somewhat more adventurous gives the opposition a glimmer of hope. Therefore, they are more likely to attack, at least for part of the innings. In this case, you might pick up a few wickets with batters attempting to score. This in turn should create more potential for wickets.

In club cricket, during two-day games, you have to bowl the side out that are batting second before you can record a win. In these circumstances, it may be preferable to declare when you have a good score on the first evening, rather than batting on to make an insurmountable target. This ensures that the opposition is constantly trying to win the game, rather than contenting themselves with a draw very early in the run chase.

Another useful time to declare in club cricket is when you have passed your opponent's score on the first day. Captains often bat on to prevent the other side from winning, but then must rely on bowling a side out whose intent is just to stay in. We always prefer to open the game up, giving the opposition a chance to gain outright points. In this case, the opposition at least have the opportunity to get some quick runs and set up a run chase for you.

The declaration of your opponents is also critical. They must give you a challenging target that keeps you going for victory right up to the end. In so doing, they hope you will lose enough wickets along the way to provide them with a chance for an outright result. This is a delicate balancing act whereby both teams must see their respective declarations as a positive sign to a win.

60

Change Bowlers Before It's Too Late

How often do we see a bowler coming to the end of a spell? His last over usually is the most costly. This often occurs because the captain has relied on blind faith rather than calculated sense, sticking with the same bowler because of his past successes.

A good captain senses the flow of a match, often making a change before others have even thought about it. These changes are intentional, showing an appreciation for the state of the game, the physical and mental conditions of the bowler, and the current (or expected) performance of the batters against particular types of bowlers.

In baseball, it is almost mandatory for the starting pitcher to be replaced in the later stages of a game, even if he has performed well. The consensus among baseball coaches is that the starting pitcher will be growing tired by the end. A relief pitcher will provide freshness and speed late in the game. In fact, they believe the change prevents an onslaught in the late innings. An offensive blitz may occur against a pitcher who has already thrown 80 pitches or so.

In light of this example, captains should appreciate their bowlers' fatigue level and should ensure that they will be fresh for a second (or possibly a third) spell. Although this method is not prescriptive for every situation, it must be at the forefront of the captain's mind, particularly with respect to front-line bowlers.

Of course, sometimes a bowler may keep going, simply because of the pressure that he is applying. This most often occurs with medium pacers or spinners, who do not show as much sign of physical weariness. The state of the game may not demand change. In fact, making a change could be exactly what the batting team wants!

Do not make double bowling changes, forcing two bowlers to settle in. This may lead to an accelerated run rate. It is wiser to stagger changes so that you don't introduce two new bowlers at the same time. In essence, be a proactive, rather than reactive, captain. Making the right change at the right time is a quality of the very best.

Respect Takes Time to Earn and Just Moments to Lose!

Coaching at any level, be it for the under 12s or on a national cricket team, is not an easy task. In addition to a thorough understanding of the requirements of each level, coaches need excellent communication skills, good planning, and sound strategies.

You do not need to have been the best player at your particular level to be a good coach. If you come to coaching with an outstanding playing record, there is no doubt that you will have respect from the start. All you can do is lose it! This is often the case when a coach struggles with communication, planning, and empathy. Good coaches earn respect by ensuring these traits are at the forefront of their coaching philosophy.

A worthwhile reminder to all coaches is the saying 'A player does not care what you know until they know that you care!' If you follow this motto, you will be on the way to earning respect.

Ricky Ponting								
	Matches	Inns	Runs	HS	BT Ave	100s	50s	Catches
Tests	146	247	12026	257	54.66	39	52	172
ODIs	351	342	13072	164	42.85	29	79	152
First-Class	246	418	20873	257	57.34	73	90	261

62

The Captain Is More Than a Figurehead

Much more is expected from cricket captains than from leaders in other sports. They must make decisions on the field that clearly affect the outcome of a game. It is easy to be a competent captain, but difficult to be a great one. The following list demonstrates the range of behaviours expected from a cricket captain. Answer the questions honestly to see how you rate with respect to mastering the art and science of captaincy.

- Can you lead by example (in terms of team values)?
- Are you a good listener?
- Do you involve others without losing your strength as a leader?
- Are you adaptable?
- Are you creative?
- Are you a risk taker?
- Are you an inspiring, confident speaker?
- Can you motivate others?
- Can you develop discipline in relation to team rules?
- Do you have a good rapport with players?
- Are you a positive role model?
- Are you courageous?
- Do you have good self-control?
- Do you have a sense of humour?
- Are you approachable?
- Can you read strengths and weaknesses in the opposition?
- Are you willing to make tough decisions?
- Are you in harmony with the coach?

- Do you have a good understanding of field placements?
- Do you give regular feedback to players?
- Are you proactive with bowling changes?
- Do you have the ability to change the momentum of the game?
- Do you maintain a positive, co-operative relationship with umpires?
- Do you have appropriate conflict-management skills?
- Are you decisive?
- Can you impart knowledge to others?

The list could go on, but we think this one demonstrates the complexity of captaining a side well. If you are a budding captain, monitor your progress on these behaviours and set goals for improving any areas of concern. Coaches should show this list to the captain to receive a rating on each, thus identifying areas where the most improvement is needed.

Jonty Rhodes									
	Matches	Inns	NO	Runs	HS	BT Ave	100s	6s	Catches
Tests	52	80	9	2532	117	35.66	3	22	34
ODIs	245	220	51	5935	121	35.11	2	47	105
First-Class	164	263	31	9546	172	41.14	22		127

63

Feel the Difference

One of the most challenging yet fundamental aspects of coaching is changing a technique. I'm sure we can all identify, either as a player or a coach, with how difficult it can be. This is perfectly understandable. In order to make a change, we essentially have to unlearn habits that have been ingrained over a long period of time.

We are often surprised at how difficult it is to change techniques. Some are harder to change than others. For example, a very talented pace bowler had suffered shin soreness for years because he placed his front foot parallel with the popping crease. We thought it would be a simple procedure to change his foot placement to point more directly down the wicket. However, this player struggled to do so, and continued to have problems with his shins. Even the possibility of reduced pain was not adequate incentive for change.

After years of trying different techniques, we have become convinced that the best path is to get athletes to feel the new technique. For instance, when working with wrist spinners who have trouble bowling wrong'uns, try positioning yourself in front of them and asking them to mimic your action. If you do this, players can instantly see the difference in their wrist position. Next, move their wrists gently but slowly through the desired positions for executing a wrong'un. Try to help them feel the technique kinaesthetically.

The same approach can be used with any cricket skill. For instance, if a batter is struggling to hit the ball through the covers because he is closing his bat face, try taking him through the way the hands work to open the bat face. This will help him develop the feel of the shot.

Become Your Own Coach

Once you are armed with the fundamentals of the game, you should be able to make adjustments whenever your technique deteriorates. The key is to look at the outcome and consider why it has occurred. The next step is to make a change that will facilitate more reliable performance of the skill.

Here are some common faults and their remedies:

Outcome 1: You are bowling too full. Typically, this results from letting the ball go a little bit early.

Adjustment. Hang on to the ball a little longer.

Outcome 2: The ball is not spinning for leg-break bowlers. Look at your hand at the moment of release. The ball is probably going out the back of your hand, creating top spin.

Adjustment. Make sure you let the ball go out the front of your hand. Point your fingers to midwicket at release. Loosen your wrist and spin the ball sideways.

Outcome 3: Hitting the ball in the air on drives. Your bottom hand might be working too much or your weight might be on your back foot at contact.

Adjustment. Do some work with your top hand. Make sure you are transferring your weight to the front foot.

In each situation, look at the difference between the actual outcome and your desired one. If there is a large and consistent discrepancy between the two, work back through the aspects of technique that could be contributing to this difference. In this way, you can train yourself to deal with technical errors as they occur. In effect, you will become your own coach.

65

What Should Coaches Expect From Their Players?

Throughout our years of coaching, we dealt with a whole range of personalities and commitment levels from players. We understand that some players may not have the same motives for playing as others. However, in order to produce quality practice sessions, it can help everyone if a bare minimum of expectations is met. From our experience, the following guidelines for players are necessary to produce high-quality training and performance:

- Make sure you psych up for each training session. Think about what you want to achieve. Become energised as you go to training. When you arrive, bounce onto the training track and get into the warm-up with enthusiasm.
- Come prepared to work on some aspect of your batting, bowling, or fielding. Ideally, this should reflect your recent performances.
- Be prepared to do more than any other team or club at this level in the country.
- Practise to improve the key areas of performance: fitness, skill, and mind control.
- Listen to or read any feedback given to you. Develop strategies with your coach for improvement.
- Be loyal to your leaders by giving a maximum effort to all drills even if you disagree with their intent or structure.

If players adhere to the preceding guidelines, coaching becomes a much easier task. Ultimately, optimal player performance is achieved.

Train as You Play

In case you haven't already realised it, it is difficult to train as you play in cricket. In fact, it is possibly the only game in the world in which net training is considered the norm and match-type training is an afterthought. For this reason, coaches must attempt to provide game-like scenarios whenever possible. Otherwise, we will continue to produce expert trainers rather than expert players.

If nets are the only option, we must set objectives and goals based on match situations. For instance, batters could be given a 60-ball challenge in which they are allowed one chance to make 40 imaginary runs. They would have to call runs and run twos appropriately. They would also be given boundaries according to the stand-in umpire (who could possibly be the next batter). The bowlers in the net would have the objective of getting two wickets for less than 40 runs. Although this may not be the real thing, it at least gets the players thinking and training with a match focus.

Plenty of other ways to set the scene in the nets exist, and the possibilities are endless. However, the coach must ensure that an actual score is recorded (possibly by the acting umpire) and that a written account of every ball is maintained. In doing this, there will always be a winner and a statistical record for analysis. The session is closer to a game than a practice session that just involves having a hit for 10 minutes.

Hopefully, the competition scenario will inadvertently teach batters the importance of balancing the value of their wicket against their own particular method of scoring. Bowlers will be forced to think about their delivery to create the desired outcome.

67

What Should Players Expect From Their Coach?

In contrast to Ian Chappell (who is both revered and provocative) and Shane Warne, we believe that a coach can offer more to the team than simply a 'ride to the ground to play cricket.' Traditionally, cricket coaches have been viewed as non-existent or subservient to captains at best. The modern approach shows a coach and captain working in harmony. Although coaches benefit from the wisdom captains have gained from experience, they can also contribute to the team. In recent times such coach-captain partnerships as John Buchanan-Steve Waugh; Gary Kirsten-M.S. Dhoni; and Andy Flower-Andrew Strauss have seemed to operate harmoniously to enhance team performance. Their trained eyes may spot trends that a captain, immersed in the emotional ebb and flow of the game, may miss from time to time. These observations and strategies, when combined with a skilful captain who is close to the action, result in the formula for planning team success.

So, what should players reasonably expect from a coach? The list may be endless, but here are some qualities that we think a good coach should demonstrate:

- Be passionate and show persistent commitment to the journey towards team success.
- Plan the overall program after consultation with players and support staff.
- Devise drills that specifically address team and individual needs.
- Set team goals.
- Guide pre-game warm-up activities that provide for individual preferences.
- Motivate the team to train and play at an optimum intensity. Model energetic and enthusiastic behaviour, even if the team is not succeeding.

- Prepare and outline goals and activities for each training session.
- Evaluate all players and give feedback following training sessions.
- Evaluate each game performance, giving feedback on positive aspects as well as identifying some areas for improvement. Provide a clear message for how this is to be achieved.
- Educate players about the intricacies of the game and encourage them to read this book!
- Be accessible to players whenever they have concerns. Be alert to changes in mood and be there to offer support when needed.
- Keep abreast of developments in sport science. Continually seek to improve the overall program. Find specific approaches to coaching players.
- Develop a program that reflects consideration of training principles and sports medicine.

Coaches who expect to just turn up and work will always fall short of the mark. As coaches become more and more accepted, expectations of players may also increase. As a player, you should respect and understand the role of the coaches while requesting them to provide you with an environment that satisfies the preceding expectations. If we all work together, coaches should provide a ride not just to the cricket ground, but also to a destination of cricket mastery.

68

Backyards and Beaches Are Great Nurseries

There is no doubt that our best learning occurs in our early years. Most parents of top-line sportsmen and women often comment on how their children threw or hit a ball from the day they could walk. In fact, most were probably catching (in some form) before they were out of the pram.

Of course, as children grow, they usually become involved in free play and backyard games that simulate the major sports they see on television. At this stage, as long as the right techniques are encouraged, children develop their awareness of games. They learn the nuances of the sport intrinsically, rather than explicitly.

For instance, they might develop a way of hitting the ball through the cover area because the backyard doesn't have any room on the leg side. Hence, they learn to get their feet in the right position and move the bat along the correct plane for a cover drive. Alternatively, they may experiment with a taped ball to learn the art of swing bowling through experience, rather than by watching a coach explain and demonstrate the correct wrist position. Even running between wickets is intrinsically learnt as players begin to appreciate the need for calling and the value of a single to keep the scoreboard ticking over. In effect, they are developing a feel for the game. A recent book titled First Tests: Great Australian Cricketers and the Backyards That Made Them, written by Steve Cannane (2010), reinforces this concept as the formative cricket years of many of the Australian greats are explored. The childhood cricket backgrounds of luminaries such as Victor Trumper, Sir Don Bradman, Clarrie Grimmett, Keith Miller, Neil Harvey, Richie Benaud, the Chappell brothers. Mike Hussey and Brett Lee (to name a few) all demonstrate both a passion for the game and an ingenuity to create games in their backyards or street that provided a foundation for their development as elite cricketers. Although correct technique is still an essential ingredient for success, intuitive learning of basic skills through random games (possibly starting in the backyard or at the beach) provides the backbone for a complete cricketer.

More-advanced cricketers should not underestimate the value of game-scenario training, as opposed to a technical session in the nets. A session with match connotations challenges players more realistically than a simple set of drills does.

The next time you are asked to take part in a backyard game, get involved and appreciate its value for beginners. You just might be starting them on the journey towards international success.

Keith Miller									
	Matches	Inns	NO	Runs	HS	BT Ave	100s	6s	Catches
Tests	55	87	7	2958	147	36.97	7	28	38
ODIs	226	326	36	14183	281	48.9	41		136
	Matches	Inns	Balls	Runs	Wkts	BT Ave	Econ	5Wkts	
Tests	55	95	10461	3906	170	22.97	2.24	7	
First-Class	226		28070	11087	497	22.3	2.36	16	

69

Coaching Wicketkeepers Is Often an Afterthought

As is the case for most coaches, wicketkeeping is not part of the game in which we feel comfortable, simply because we haven't had to do it. We appreciate them, but often we are only attracted to keepers if they make a mistake. When you watch the ball, you seldom focus on the keeper, making it difficult to give worthwhile feedback.

When we were nearing the nervous nineties in the production of this book, we became acutely aware that we were neglecting wicketkeeping. It is an important part of field performance. We then decided that it would be useful to give our thoughts on what we looked for in keepers. We hope to identify a core of principles to help novice wicketkeeping coaches such as ourselves. Check out the following key points and see where your keeper sits.

A competent wicketkeeper has the following qualities:

- Sets the standard in the field with enthusiasm, voice, and commitment to ball-by-ball focus
- Has a strong work ethic and continually employs drills that can be practised in small groups
- Consults a mentor with experience in keeping from time to time during the season
- Can take the ball with soft hands
- Can keep up to the stumps for pace bowlers
- Is courageous enough to keep watching the ball even when there is a flurry of bat and arms from the batter
- Has quick footwork for every ball of every day
- Can take the ball on the inside thigh
- Practises diving so that it becomes a habit (Catching in soft sand or into a high jump bag is a useful practice for this skill component.)

- Does a shoulder roll when diving for catches
- Waits for the ball to bounce before coming up from the crouch or semi-crouch position
- Accelerates up to the wicket after every hit shot from the batter
- Practises taking both poor throws and good ones to prepare to execute run-outs when they are offered
- Has mobility, leg power, and endurance
- Can read the spin of the ball as it leaves the spinner's hand

In general, a wicketkeeper sets the standard for defensive work. Therefore, don't understate or undervalue it just because you haven't done it.

Adam Gilchrist									
	Matches	Inns	NO	Runs	HS	BT Ave	100s	Catches	ST
Tests	96	137	20	5570	204	47.6	17	379	37
ODIs	287	279	11	9619	172	35.89	16	417	55
T20Is	13	13	1	272	48	22.66	0	17	0
First-Class	190	280	46	10334	204	44.16	30	756	55
Twenty20	68	68	2	1773	109	26.86	2	48	19

General

lthough cricket is a simple game, more often than not, it requires a lot of smarts to win. It is not merely a game that involves one team making more runs than the other. Success requires much more than mastering the fundamentals. This section explores a host of aspects that will make you a smarter cricketer.

In addition to the ability to display the techniques, you must have a strong and focused mind in order to be consistently successful. Players today need to balance offence and defence at various times within a game. They need to be versatile and adaptable to different conditions or game states. Practices should be specifically aimed at remedying flaws that have occurred in the games. The ability to confront higher challenges and to cope with losses of form is paramount in continuing to grow as a player. Individual ability and smarts contribute to success, but teamwork ultimately determines the results of games. Watching and learning from others is also very important in maintaining continual improvement. The culture of cricket clubs can play a huge part in retaining players. Young players may be intimidated by the behaviour of senior players and may actually stop playing because of the treatment they receive.

We decided to add our own short stories. We hope they have a useful message for players and coaches. Neil outlines how much he learned from being involved in successful teams over his career. Ken describes in vivid detail how a team of country players he captained coped with the might of the West Indies when they were at their most powerful.

We hope you enjoy the challenge of adding some of these approaches to your game.

It's Not Offensive to Be Defensive!

C ricket, like most games, is about balancing offence with defence in a sensible manner. It is particularly difficult to strike a satisfactory balance in batting. If you are aggressive and you get out, coaches will argue that you have erred. The current philosophy in cricket is to be aggressive at all times. With run rates constantly being presented, young cricketers can be excused for going all-out on the attack.

However, even the most aggressive batters know the value of defending. At times, bowlers deliver balls that are too threatening to attempt to score. Players who continue to try to thrash bowlers are almost certain to have their innings curtailed by a clever one. For example, if two slashing drives have been played through mid-off for boundaries, a ball delivered wider and fuller is potentially dangerous for an in-form batter. It should be left alone.

The same principle applies to bowlers. You don't need to attack a batter all the time to get a wicket. In one-day cricket, bowlers sometimes get too defensive, losing sight of the value of gaining a wicket by slowing down batting momentum. However, bowlers who are patient in all forms of cricket build pressure on batters, often facilitating an error. New Zealand's Daniel Vettori is a master in all forms of the game. He dries up batters and creates wickets through guile and an essentially defensive mindset. This combination of attack and defence is a constant dilemma for cricket players. If you strike the right balance, you will be on the track to success. Favouring one to the exclusion of the other is a recipe for failure.

71

Learn From Mistakes, Don't Repeat Them

We are never too old to learn. Improvement requires either bettering our skills, fitness, and mental approach or by resolving to avoid the same mistakes. For example, you might have been dismissed trying to hit a six over the head of a boundary fielder. Next time, try to hit singles or twos when there are four fielders on the fence. If you have been out leg before wicket when playing across the line, you should commit to playing straighter when next you bat.

Here are some examples for bowlers. If you have bowled short on a slow wicket and have been punished, you should recognise that situation when next it occurs and adapt accordingly. If you have bowled to a 7-2 field and have tried to bounce a batter who has hooked you for four, then perhaps you should consider field placements that are more appropriate before attempting such a strategy again.

When fielding, if you throw the ball short of the target from your position in the covers, then your next throw should be aimed higher. Similarly, if you drop a catch in slips because your hands are going down at the point of contact, then you should modify your starting position to accommodate more knee bend. This will bring your hands lower.

In summary, a host of learning experiences can be gained from every performance. Don't go into your shell and end up doing nothing. Learn from your mistakes, work on correcting them, and adjust your approach accordingly.

Silent Nights Are Golden

The quality of training is sometimes diminished if there is constant chatter between players. Cricket training is usually replete with a host of players who stir others good naturedly or talk between deliveries about their conquests on the weekend (on or off the field). This often means that a bowler's focus drifts from the essential task of planning, executing, and evaluating each delivery. Players simply walk back while chatting to another player, and then turn and run in to bowl without giving the delivery any attention. Hence, bowling plans cease and practice becomes more a case of going through the motions.

Abdul Qadir, a sublimely skilful spinner for Pakistan, remarked that he wanted to be in his own concentrated world when he trained. Phil Jackson, famous former coach of the Chicago Bulls (which included the legendary Michael Jordan), conducted whole practices in silence. He was astonished by the deep level of concentration and non-verbal communication that such practice evoked.

Lead your club into the cone of silence from time to time and reap the benefits.

Abdul Qadir								
	Matches	Inns	Balls	Runs	Wkts	BT Ave	Econ	5Wkts
Tests	67	111	17126	7742	236	32.8	2.71	15
ODIs	104	100	5100	3454	132	26.16	4.06	2
First-Class	209		49036	22314	960	23.24	2.73	75

73

Do More

We once came across a quote from an unnamed source that talked about doing more. We have expanded this idea, adding some of our own advice that relates to competitive sport. Don't take this advice too literally. Overzealous players need to be wary of the philosophy that more is always better. (If 300 bowls a week are good, then 400 are obviously better!) Clearly, with the incidence of overuse injuries, you need to be suspicious of such a philosophy. Follow guidelines that are less simplistic and listen to your body. However, many young cricketers clearly do not put in the time needed to ingrain their foundational skills.

With this need for balance in mind, we present the following list for you to digest and ponder in your cricket life:

- Do more than exist—live.
- Do more than look—observe.
- Do more than read—absorb. (Are you absorbing this message?)
- Do more than hear—listen.
- Do more than listen—understand.
- Do more than think—ponder.
- Do more than plan—act.
- Do more than talk—say something.
- Do more than participate—compete.
- Do more than be a member—contribute.
- Do more than be involved—commit.

If you do more of these, you can rest assured that your coach will be impressed by your attitude to self-improvement. Some of these statements are more appropriate to cricket than others, but they will all contribute to your improvement as a player if you commit to their message.

Come to Practise, Don't Turn Up for Practice

I t is impossible for a coach to devise training sessions that meet your needs perfectly every time. Many competing factors must be considered when designing a practice. Which would you choose in each of the following examples?

- Team requirements or individual needs
- Physical fitness, practical skills, or mental skills
- Match conditions or repetitive skill practice
- Some variety to rejuvenate players and add fun to a session or the same drills every time
- Modest load to prevent injuries or overload to challenge players

With this in mind, players must own their training needs and come prepared to do more if their needs are not met at a session. For instance, if a spin bowler feels at the end of a session on Thursday night that he has not had enough bowling, then he should commit to doing extra work either after training or on Friday evening on his own.

In addition to taking more ownership, players need to make sure they are motivated to train at their peak. You should spend some time before training to consider your goals for a session and psych yourself up to train well, no matter what the coach directs you to do. We often hear players complaining about how they lack motivation to practise. Remember, you have to work at controlling your mental state. You can choose to be either enthusiastic or lethargic. If you choose the former, you have a chance to maximise every training session.

75

Concentrate!

You often hear this catch-cry when watching cricket, but you rarely see coaches giving guidance on how to concentrate. What is concentration and how can you improve it?

Most athletes can recall a performance when they were in the zone or in a state of flow. Everything became easy and nothing seemed to worry them. They felt in control, focusing appropriately for the whole performance. They were neither worried about past performance nor thinking about the future—they were simply in the present, playing each ball or moment with optimal focus.

This ideal performance state is not always easy to achieve. We frequently allow opposition players to distract us, thinking about their comments as the next delivery is bowled. Sometimes we determine how we are going to play a shot before it is bowled. Occasionally, we start thinking about what it will be like to win a game, imagining the celebrations before the task has been completed. Bowlers may be dwelling on a previous poor delivery as they prepare to bowl another. All of these situations reflect an inappropriate focus. They have the potential for dire consequences.

Being aware of these lapses is the first step to improving your concentration. Whenever this happens, you should develop a process for ensuring that your mind is clear and that you are prepared to play the next delivery with optimal focus.

For a batter, it is useful to set small goals. Don't focus too far into the future. Watch the ball closely as the bowler runs in to bowl. Say 'now' to yourself as the ball leaves the bowler's hands, triggering your body and mind to get ready. Be ready to pounce on any delivery in your hitting zone, but also be prepared to defend if necessary.

If you are having lots of lapses in concentration, it may be useful for you to track the ball for a period of time. Watch it hit the wicketkeeper's gloves as you leave the ball. Track it as it passes from fielder to fielder en route back to the bowler. Do not worry about previous deliveries or get too far ahead of yourself. Essentially, whenever you notice your focus drifting, pull it back by watching the ball and saying a cue word to yourself that will help you refocus. Examples include 'play straight,' 'move your feet,' or 'be positive!'

When bowling, concentration lapses may be due to lack of thought about what you are going to bowl. You simply turn, run in, and let it go. You may still be thinking about the previous delivery, ruing your bad luck at a missed catch or an umpire's decision. You could also be engaged in verbal warfare with a batter.

Whatever the cause of the distraction, you need to be able to focus on the next ball. The process should involve a brief review of the previous delivery (Why did you bowl a full toss?). Next, forget about the past delivery and focus on the type you are going to bowl next. Take a deep breath, imagine how you are going to bowl, and look at the spot you're aiming for. Run in with a cue word in your mind ('strong,' 'relax,' or 'smooth'). Let it happen, and watch the stumps fly out of the ground.

The best focus for fielders and wicketkeepers is to prepare for every ball to come to them. If you do this with full intensity, maintaining soft hands, you should be able to execute your skills optimally.

Richie Benaud									
	Matches	Inns	NO	Runs	HS	BT Ave	100s	6s	Catches
Tests	63	97	7	2201	122	24.45	3	8	65
First-Class	259	365	44	11719	187	36.5	23		254
	Matches	Inns	Balls	Runs	Wkts	BT Ave	Econ	5Wkts	
Tests	63	116	19108	6704	248	27.03	2.1	16	
First-Class	259		60481	23370	945	24.73	2.31	56	

76

Game-Like Training

I t sounds simple, doesn't it? However, when we watch people training, we continually see coaches and players ignoring the specificity principle. In simple terms, this means that you should aim to train as closely as possible to game situations. Granted, it is difficult to create training activities that replicate game situations in cricket. Still, this should not deter committed coaches. A simple example of this problem is that you often have only 10 minutes to bat at practice, yet are often asked to bat for many hours in a game. It is not easy to train specifically for match conditions, but with some thought, you can better approximate game situations.

The following training habits are not specific:

- Facing a spin bowler for one ball, then contending with a pace bowler for the next delivery
- Fielding a ball that is hit to you with a flat bat and returning it in a direct line from whence it came (No one except the bowler has to field that type of hit.)
- Failing to notice where the fielders are placed when batting in the nets
- Hitting the ball in the air without fear of consequences
- Nicking a ball to the wicketkeeper and staying in (Unless he drops the catch, of course!)
- Failing to run between deliveries when batting
- Bowling repeatedly for an hour at a time (We bowl for six deliveries and rest for six, so we should practice under these conditions.)
- Batting without a target score in mind
- Bowling no balls continually at training (The flight path of a ball delivered from 19 metres is different from one delivered legally.)
- Practising slips catching with a horizontal bat (Many slips catches occur after a stroke from a vertical angle.)

Although you can never perfectly replicate a game situation, aim to structure training in accordance with match conditions. Specificity of training remains a constant challenge for both coaches and players.

Matthew Hayden									
	Matches	Inns	NO	Runs	HS	BT Ave	100s	6s	Catches
Tests	103	184	14	8625	380	50.73	30	82	128
ODIs	161	155	15	6133	181	43.8	10	87	68
T20Is	9	9	3	308	73	51.33	0	13	1
First-Class	295	515	47	24603	380	52.57	79		296
Twenty20	41	41	5	1415	93	39.3	0	57	12

77

Bring on the Spotlights: Tips for Playing in Finals

Finals are usually played at an elevated level, so be ready for more intensity. Let the thought challenge and excite you. Don't be fearful or worried about the outcome. The following tips will help you prepare for finals:

- Practise with intensity, particularly in the field. Do extra fielding sessions so that you are confident you can attack the ball, pick up cleanly, and throw strongly under any level of pressure. Make fielding practice competitive to create pressure.

- Practise catching. Expect to take a catch each time rather than just hoping that you will. Increase catching practice in the weeks preceding finals.

- Try to create specific fielding drills. That is, if you field at short cover, have the batter hit catches and ground balls at the same angle.

- Do extra work as the pinnacle of the season approaches, then taper into quality sessions as you enter the finals.

- Make sure you know how you play best. Commit to making that approach work for you in finals. Do not make major changes heading into finals.

- Channel nervous energy into determination by focusing on doing your task well and resolving to never give in.

- If you are in good form, be confident, but expect the game to be tough when you get in. Conversely, if you are in bad form, convince yourself that you are due to play well and that you have not lost your ability. The big stage is all you need!

- Show the opposition at all times that you are focused and on a mission. Your collective sense of team should unnerve the opposition. Even if you are down, this aspect should always shine through.

- Have confidence in your preparation and your readiness to accept the upcoming challenge. Relax during the days preceding the game. Minimise conflicts at work or home and start to get into your own cocoon. Visualise key aspects that will make you successful, and then switch off thoughts of the game. You do not want to have played your game before you get to the ground.
- Prepare to be strong in your mind. Courage, patience, determination, and focus must be at their peak. You may lose because you are not good enough on the day, but you should never lose the battle of the mind. Preparing for elevated levels of intensity can assist players to be ready for finals' games. Remember that you are there because you deserve to be, focus on giving your best effort and the result will hopefully take care of itself.

Andy Flower								
	Matches	Inns	NO	Runs	HS	BT Ave	100s	Catches
Tests	63	112	19	4794	232	51.54	12	151
ODIs	213	208	16	6786	145	35.34	4	141
First-Class	223	372	69	16379	271	54.05	49	361
List A	380	366	45	12511	145	38.97	12	254
Twenty20	21	20	2	595	83	33.05	0	6

The Power of the Leading Arm

I t is not surprising that youngsters often minimise the input from their leading arm in cricket techniques. You don't throw or bowl with your leading arm, so isn't it logical to give it a rest in your technique practice? Not so!

In throwing and bowling, you need to initiate the movement with strong use of the front arm. In the throw, the front arm tends toward the target, and then thrusts vigorously into the rib cage as the throwing arm starts to move forward. Similarly, in bowling, the leading arm is raised high so that it can also thrust into the rib cage as the action unfolds.

In batting, the leading arm is critical for success. It should be aligned with the intended direction of straight-batted shots. If the elbow flaps around to the side, considerable power and direction can be lost. This technique of a high, powerful front elbow is difficult for many to achieve, since it is often on the non-preferred side of their body. That is, right-handed batters who throw with the right hand or left-handed batters who throw with the left hand are at somewhat of a disadvantage here.

An interesting fact is that many of our best left-handed batters are right-hand dominant. Some examples include Adam Gilchrist, Matthew Hayden, Chris Gayle, Graeme Smith, Alastair Cook, and Michael Hussey.

However, no matter which is your dominant hand, if you train the front arm in batting, the force will be with you.

There's No *I* in 'Team'

Cricket is interesting because it is an individual game played by members of a team. While batting, a player can clearly bat to stay in for as long as possible. This may or may not be in the best interests of the team. Individual achievements, such as batting and bowling averages, can often hinder your total commitment to the team.

Everyone has played with someone highly motivated who appears to have prioritised individual interests at the expense of team goals. If their ability matches their intent, they can be seen as the top performers in a team. However, if they aren't doing absolutely everything for the team, then they are setting it up for failure.

Some specific examples can clarify this point. We have often played against batters who, when chasing a sizeable tally like 300, seem to be content with walking off the ground unconquered on 75 while the team has scored 250 runs. Sure, they have top scored, but they have not been willing to play some higher risk shots to break up the game and catapult their team score over the 300 mark. In essence, in-form batters should be the one most capable of increasing the scoring rate. Therefore, they should take responsibility for leading the assault on the opposition's tally. The fundamental principle is to try to win the game. Any individual performances are mere stepping stones in achieving team success.

On occasions when playing for a draw, a batter may try to score more runs than are needed, satisfying ego at the expense of optimal team performance. Batters are not the only ones who can destroy team ethos. Bowlers can often become petulant when they are taken off. Sometimes leading bowlers dictate which end they will bowl from to the captain. They might also bowl in an attacking manner when the plan is to contain the batters. Fielders can also be individually focused, unaware of the importance of concentration for team success. If you don't prepare as if every ball will be hit to you, you are letting the team down.

The key is to have the team in mind at all times. Enjoy the fruits that team harmony and cohesion can bring to achieving the ultimate prize.

80

Be in the Team, Not Just on the Team Sheet

Just because you are selected to be on a cricket team does not mean you are in the team. You are only in once you are accepted by others in the team as a player who unquestionably exhibits team behaviours over and above any quest for individual achievement. Many of these team attributes are developed at training. Check out the following list to see where you sit.

Team players do the following:

- They turn up to all training sessions This sounds simple, but many players just happen to go missing when a tough training session is planned.

- They think about their specific role in the next game and practice accordingly. For example, they might be asked to open the batting in a one-day game with the purpose of getting the side off to an aggressive start. In preparation, they practice hitting the ball over the infield and playing shots to the safest spots on the field.

- They are proactive in doing additional exercises because they don't want to let the team down by being underprepared. They want their skills to stand up under pressure.

- They practise at optimum level of intensity at all times.

- They take pride in their appearance while complying with team apparel designed for training.

- At training, they encourage others to perform at their peak.

- They help set up for training and pack up as needed.

- They handle any selection disappointment in a positive manner.

- They are aware of other players' needs and assist them where appropriate.

- They make sure that practice is competitive, but they are aware of other players whose confidence may be down. Therefore, they may not always go all out to dismiss or intimidate a batter on inferior practice wickets.

It is exhilarating to train with a team of players who exhibit the preceding behaviours. The sense of shared purpose is far more satisfying than individual success.

Kapil Dev									
	Matches	Inns	NO	Runs	HS	BT Ave	100s	6s	Catches
Tests	131	184	15	5248	163	31.05	8	61	64
ODIs	225	198	39	3783	175	23.79	1		71
First-Class	275	384	39	11356	193	32.91	18		192
List A	310	270	47	5481	175	24.57	2		99
	Matches	Inns	Balls	Runs	Wkts	BT Ave	5Wkts		
Tests	131	227	27740	12867	434	29.64	23		
ODIs	225	221	11202	6945	253	27.45	1		
First-Class	275		48853	22626	835	27.09	39		
List A	310		14947	9161	335	27.34	2		

81

Team Behaviour on Game Day

I remember clearly a Test cricketer from about a decade ago who warmed up for his club side in his national gear. I am still aghast at how a player could do that whilst considering himself part of the team. Of course, this person may have been a great team player, but the message he sent to his team-mates was that he was above the rest of them, that he didn't have to comply with team needs. I would have thought that a Test player would recognise this blatant elitism, doing everything he could to be seen as a team player.

(Ken Davis)

In the previous chapter we spoke of how a player can exhibit team behaviours at training and in general around the club. On game day it is also vital that players can focus on both their own games and their team's needs. The following guidelines can help ensure players are able to do the little things that enhance team performance.

Off the field when your team is batting, a team player does the following:

- Tries to be part of the group, mingling with others, regardless of his own performances
- Shows up on time
- Dresses in team apparel
- Genuinely enjoys other players' successes
- Uses his voice to encourage teammates throughout the day

On the field, a team player does the following:

- Takes responsibility for keeping team enthusiasm high, particularly when the side is down

- Displays energy between overs (jogs to position, gives bowlers a pat on the back)
- Acknowledges desperate efforts in the field
- Bats with courage under fire
- When threatened physically, consistently gets in line with the ball, even if there is risk of being hit
- Bats to a team tally, not to his own
- Bowls tightly or aggressively, depending on the situation
- Stays in tune with what the team is trying to achieve (In the field, the captain may be trying to keep one of the batters on strike, so awareness is important here.)
- Works hard, even if his previous involvement in the game has not been personally productive or satisfying

We hope you come to realise that the team's performance is the ultimate measuring stick. Do everything in your power to be seen as a team player!

82

Play Other Sports

For some time now, we have supported the increasingly unpopular view that players should be encouraged to play other sports, even at the elite level. There seems to be a powerful belief that more is always better: If you can practice for 365 days a year instead of 250, then you will automatically become better at your skills. Better still, why not practice two or three times a day? That is, if you can stay awake!

Our view is that you should delay specialisation until it is apparent that you have made the grade at senior level and have established a clear career path. Playing other sports can help in so many ways. You must not shut out other recreational pursuits at an early age.

First, other physical activities can provide psychological benefits. Cricket is typically a summer game, which allows time for other choices. Another sport that is completely divergent can refresh players in the off season. Sports that are different from cricket, such as tennis, hockey, basketball, baseball, lacrosse, and football, may provide some competitive insights that players can transfer to cricket.

Second, by playing another sport, players will maintain an active regimen of training and match preparation, albeit at a reduced level of intensity or expectation. Sometimes, it's good just to play and enjoy physical activity, without playing for sheep stations. Serious athletes appreciate getting their exercise in an enjoyable way, rather than pounding the pavement all the time in pre-season.

Of course, in some instances, the risk of injury may outweigh the benefits. Some negative effects of transfer between the two sports may also occur. Notwithstanding these issues, we think young athletes should be encouraged to participate in at least two sports, continuing with them until a professional pathway is clearly established. Coaches are challenged to manage these athletes so that they can explore programs in both sports.

Practise
With Distractions

We are often alarmed when players tell people to move from behind the bowler's arm at practice. In fact, players should practise with all manner of distractions present to prepare for any situation that may occur in a game. If you are a batter, the process is rather simple. Watch the bowler's action closely and zero in on the ball after it leaves his hand. Nothing else should distract you from this primary focus. You should be so centred on the essentials and the execution of the shot that you scarcely notice any movement or change in the background.

In reality, typical net training provides the ideal opportunity for practising your concentration. With bowlers operating in the surrounding nets, the noise of bat on ball from the adjacent net, and plenty of fielding action in the background, the scenario is perfect for tuning in your mind.

You can practise this skill in other sport and life situations. For example, at a party you can try to focus completely on the words and facial expressions of one person (it might help if this person is attractive to you!) while others are talking in the group. If you can take in every word this person says, then your ability to handle distractions is enhanced. You might also be engaged in a game of social tennis with players on adjoining courts. Practise continuing to play, even when a ball from a nearby court drifts into your line of vision.

The idea is to continually train yourself to perform any task with distractions present. Doing so will help you cope with a myriad of things that are used either deliberately or inadvertently to get your mind off the essentials of the task. So, embrace distraction and strengthen your ability to deal with it whenever it may occur.

84

When to Watch the Players, Not the Ball

*S*ome years ago, I went to the Australian Open with my daughter Brooke, who was about 9 years old and just starting out in tennis. It would be fair to say her footwork at that time, like most novices, left a little to be desired. At this event we were privileged to observe the dancing feet of Steffi Graf. I can recall saying to Brooke, 'Let's just watch Steffi's feet for five minutes.' From that day on, Brooke's footwork improved tremendously, and she still uses this cue whenever her game is off the boil.

(Ken Davis)

Watching the ball closely is surely fundamental to our game, so why would someone watch the player? In simple terms, we do so to optimise learning. When you think about it, you are actually a spectator much of the time in cricket. You may have been dismissed early and must sit with the team for up to six hours. You may be fielding, but have been in the action for only seven deliveries in the entire day.

Many people waste an opportunity to learn from the performance on display, merely looking at the game rather than closely analysing the players' techniques. It is rather like observing a panoramic view like a waterfall. We take in the overall effect before selecting parts of the view that are more interesting. It is only then that we start to appreciate the awesome power of the water as it plunges to the rocks below.

How should you watch a game? Consider the previous example about watching tennis that illustrates the preferred approach. What happened there is that we watched the player rather than watching the ball, as spectators typically do. In cricket, train yourself to watch the player. Do not be too fussed with the overall perspective. Look for the following the next time you play or watch an elite game:

- The players' grip of the bat and their backlift (See if you can work out which shots may be difficult for them to play.)

- The batters' footwork (Do they move forward or back? Is this movement initiated before or after the ball leaves the bowler's hand? What type of delivery might cause them trouble? For example, if the player moves forward all the time, might a bouncer be a wise option?)

- The starting positions of fielders and how much ground they cover from the start of a bowler's run up to the delivery (What happens after the ball is hit to them? How low do they get down? How much give is in their hands? Where does the arm go in preparation for the throw? Watch their feet as they get in position to throw.)

- The fielders who do not field the ball (Watch their movement to back up and support.)

- Fielders who are good and those who are poorer (Train yourself so that this identification becomes instinctive when you go out to bat. Who throws left-handed? Which fielder could you best sneak a single to?)

- The action of a bowler to see if you can discern any differences in either their run-up or delivery

These are just a few examples of how you can learn by really watching. When next you view a game, by all means, be entertained. However, from time to time, put on your watcher's hat and use the experience to expand your knowledge and understanding of our great game.

85

Grow a Tree That Produces Fruit Every Year

Ken recently gave a talk to a promising group of young cricketers about performance keys in cricket. He wanted to illustrate that performance outcomes are the result of several processes because so many things can improve performance. His brief was to see if he could identify the keys for them.

As is his wont, he spent some time thinking about how he might present this topic in a way that would capture their attention and aid retention. Driving up the highway, he came upon the notion of a performance tree. In the seminar, he drew a somewhat primitive tree and divided it into four segments:

1. The root system, which is ever growing
2. The ground surface, which needs constant nurturing
3. The trunk, which must remain firm, deal with the elements, and serve as the link between the roots and the branches
4. The branches and the foliage

He then asked himself and the group to label these segments in terms of overall performance. He guided them by starting at the top, saying that the foliage is the final outcome. It is what we see first when we look at an attractive eucalypt or jacaranda. The flowers and the leaves are the runs, wickets, catches, run-outs, and so on. Here is what the group came up with:

Performance Tree

- *Foliage.* The leaves and flowers signify runs, etcetera.
- *Top of the trunk where branches start.* This section is game smarts and tactical awareness.

- *Trunk.* This section symbolises courage, attack and defence, consistency, control, work ethic, consistency, and concentration. It also includes the ability to change momentum, read and exploit opposition, and thrive on pressure .
- *Ground surface.* This portion is for nutrition, preparation, and recovery.
- *Roots.* This strong, ever-growing system makes up the foundation of performance and includes skill, technique, fitness, and mental strength.

The group was then asked to use these keys to set goals for the season and to appraise their performance. In so doing, they were awakened to how performance outcomes can be improved by paying attention to a host of factors.

Michael Clarke								
	Matches	Inns	Runs	HS	BT Ave	100s	50s	Catches
Tests	62	101	4514	168	50.71	14	19	61
ODIs	178	162	5509	130	43.03	4	42	69
T20Is	33	27	472	67	21.45	0	1	13
First-Class	120	204	8475	201	46.05	28	34	118

86

Taking It One Step at a Time

eing elevated to a higher level in sport is an inspiring thought, but success is rarely accomplished without some form of adjustment to the increased physical and psychological demands of the new level. In professional sport, coaches and the media don't often understand the difficulty in going from Third XI-grade cricket to the firsts, from grade cricket to state, and from state to international cricket.

Sometimes, players are awestruck by the quality of cricketers in their own or opposing teams. Imagine what it would be like for a young cricketer to play his first game alongside Ricky Ponting or Andrew Flintoff, whom they may have idolised as a child. Naturally, they would feel less comfortable and less accepted in the new surroundings, provoking such self-doubting thoughts as 'Am I good enough to be here? Will I make a fool of myself?'

We don't expect to climb a ladder for the first time by going straight to the top. Instead, we go one cautious step at a time. Even if you slip a little from time to time, stay intent on securing a foothold before committing to the next step.

Our message to coaches and players is to be aware of the challenge of adapting to a new level. Players should aim to simplify their task, not complicate it, by focusing on the fundamentals that have gained them selection. Expect to be intimidated and expect a higher level of intensity. Still, trust your skills. These specific guidelines will help you cope when you are next faced with playing at a higher level:

- When batting, have a clear and positive game plan. Don't be overly cautious, but don't try to play every shot in the book from the start of your innings, either.
- Play the ball, not the bowler. Make positive actions with your feet.
- Be patient and calm, but not negative.

- Get off strike if you can. Call loudly and decisively.
- Once you're over the initial hump, set small goals.
- For bowlers, commit to a relaxation strategy at the top of your mark and focus on the spot you are aiming at to direct the ball.
- If a catch comes to you, be purposeful but relaxed. Let the ball come to you. When anxious, a player's tendency is to push his hands at the ball.
- Desire the ball to come to you in the field.

Above all, use the occasion to become accustomed to the surrounds. Let yourself perform one step at a time.

Chris Gayle									
	Matches	Inns	NO	Runs	HS	BT Ave	100s	6s	Catches
Tests	88	155	6	6007	317	40.31	12	66	84
ODIs	220	215	15	7885	153	39.42	19	165	95
T20Is	20	20	1	617	117	32.47	1	34	5
First-Class	162	288	21	11761	317	44.04	28		142
Twenty20	51	50	5	1357	117	30.15	1	74	17

87

When Things Are Going Badly, Think of the Forest After a Fire

I can remember driving over a fire-ravaged region in Victoria, after the infamous Ash Wednesday fires in 1982. I couldn't believe the desolation. Yet not long after, I visited the area again. Although the forest had been devastated and reduced to a shadow of its former splendour, already trees and shrubs were sprouting fresh growth. The forest fought back almost immediately and regenerated healthy new foliage in a very short period of time.
(Ken Davis)

OK, so you've had a bad run of late. You can't seem to get bat on ball. When you do, you nick it, and it goes straight through to the wicketkeeper's eager gloves. You seem to lack rhythm and consistency with your bowling. All your indicators of progress are spiralling downwards into a seemingly bottomless pit. There seems to be no way out, and your confidence and enthusiasm for cricket is waning at a rapid rate. How do you turn the tide?

Cricketers can learn much from the powers of nature. When devastated, don't just wallow in your disappointment; get back to basics and start growing again. Initially, it can be beneficial to commit yourself to a fitness program. Physical strength and well-being are usually associated with gains in confidence and self-image. So, get active and see if you can sprout some new growth.

The next step is to explore your game and identify some possible causes for your decline. Is it a technical issue or a mental one? Once you have identified the problem, set a specific program into motion to correct it. Although many of these processes appear in other sections of this book, you need to proactively address these problem areas. Remember, you don't lose your ability overnight. Trust your remedial program.

The Power of Peer Assessment

Your fellow players are closer to the action than the coaches are, so they can sometimes gain greater insights into your play. In a strong team environment, an astute coach can utilise the power of your peer group to highlight aspects of your game that warrant attention. The final message a player receives may not be any different from the coach's observations. However, if it is given by fellow players, it might be seen as more potent.

If you disagree with a coach's assessment, you may fail to address the concerns. However, if 90 percent of the other players think that you are guilty of playing too extravagantly early in your innings, then there is nowhere for you to hide.

This process has been used with good effect in several teams that were already quite advanced in their commitment to each other. They were relatively successful, but were looking to take the next step. To achieve this, a comprehensive analysis chart was developed that asked players to rank each other on all aspects. Finally, a summary of key findings was collated. This information was presented to each player.

This is a delicate process. You don't want this to look like a witch hunt. Players need to be both honest and tactful in their assessment. It is best to keep responses anonymous so that personal conflicts don't occur.

Michael Clarke								
	Matches	Inns	Runs	HS	BT Ave	100s	50s	Catches
Tests	62	101	4514	168	50.71	14	19	61
ODIs	178	162	5509	130	43.03	4	42	69
T20Is	33	27	472	67	21.45	0	1	13
First-Class	120	204	8475	201	46.05	28	34	118

89

Playing With Pain Is a Balancing Act

I n our time in cricket, we have witnessed considerable changes in the area of injury diagnosis and rehabilitation. In bygone years, bowlers seldom missed games, often soldiering on throughout a season with constant soreness in their backs, groins, or shoulders. Pain was an inevitable and constant companion of pace bowlers.

Now we have sophisticated technology that can more accurately diagnose specific injuries. Athletes are better educated on the risks of overuse and unaccustomed-use injuries. Such education may predispose athletes to quit training whenever a little, niggling ache occurs in the body. Most physiotherapists adopt a conservative view, encouraging players to report any soreness to them. A player armed with this information may often miss training sessions. The likely result is that the physical requirements of the training program are not met.

We must learn to strike a balance between the uninformed body bashing of yesteryear and the somewhat constrained view of today that tends to wrap players in cotton wool. By all means, utilise advanced medical and training techniques. However, let's beware of the medical-room malingerer. Flush him out onto the playing field! Tolerating low levels of pain is necessary if you wish to prepare yourself adequately for competitive cricket.

Our advice to young cricketers is to be prepared to play with some pain, If pain persists, see your doctor!

Jonty Rhodes									
	Matches	Inns	NO	Runs	HS	BT Ave	100s	6s	Catches
Tests	52	80	9	2532	117	35.66	3	22	34
ODIs	245	220	51	5935	121	35.11	2	47	105
First-Class	164	263	31	9546	172	41.14	22		127

Evaluating Performance: Moving Beyond Statistics

Cricket is a game of statistics. With batting, we compile lists of runs scored, averages, partnerships, and scoring rates. With bowling, we equate good performances with the number of wickets taken, economy rates, and strike rates. Although these figures provide a tangible record of a player's performance over time, they can sometimes mask his real contribution in a particular game.

For instance, if a batter is involved in a 50- or 100-run partnership, but is only a minor contributor with respect to his individual score, his importance can be easily brushed aside. Similarly, an opening batter who weathers the storm on a tough wicket but who misses out on the scoreboard may help set up the middle order by denting the effect of the new ball.

With respect to bowling, a player who might not take a wicket but who keeps pressure on the batters by maintaining a good line and length may in fact contribute to the wickets when the opposition batters try and score off the other bowlers.

Also, a player's contribution in the field is often undervalued, particularly when statistics are not recorded for runs saved or run-outs achieved. Ideally, values should be given to players who either save runs or have a high percentage of conversions with catches and run-outs. These players are invaluable in any team.

When evaluating a performance, be careful not to undervalue a player's performance. The stolen run in the latter stages of a one-day game, the knock-down in the field which saves a boundary, or the six excellently delivered yorkers in the 50th over may mean more to the result than what you read in the scorebook.

91

Versatility in an Increasingly Specialised World

In contemporary society, we have witnessed a trend towards specialisation in so many aspects of human endeavour. In years gone by, we took our cars to a local mechanic, but now we go to a brake specialist and a muffler man. We now use a general practitioner as a reference for all manner of specialists, from eye and ear doctors to skin and foot professionals.

In many sports, particularly in America, these trends have been mirrored. For example, in American football a squad of 80 players can be rotated among 11 positions on the field at the whim of the coaching staff. Specialist kickers may only spend three minutes on the field on a good day! Baseball players have a pitching rotation that involves the role of a specialist finisher, whose task is usually limited to the last couple of innings.

Throughout our involvement in the game, cricket seems to have gone through phases. In the 1960s, an abundance of fast bowlers could scarcely hold a bat. These players were less than average in the field. However, all-rounders, such as Keith Miller, Kapil Dev, Richie Benaud, Sir Ian Botham, and the peerless Sir Garfield Sobers, seemed to enrich teams so much that a quest for complete cricketers was always on the agenda.

In this period, many still felt that to develop all-round skill was to minimise the chances of mastering a particular skill. Jim Higgs, the former Australian leg-spinner, maintained that in order to master his craft, he couldn't afford the time needed to become expert at fielding or batting. However, in this age of professionalism, time is no longer a consideration.

Also, the modern game almost demands that players have skills in at least two of the main areas of the game. Recent cricket history is replete with examples of tail-end batters figuring in substantial partnerships. Brett Lee, Harbhajan Singh, and Daniel Vettori readily come to mind as players who have almost become all-rounders after first establishing themselves as bowlers. Batters such as Darren Lehmann, Sachin Tendulkar, and Chris Gayle have also taken vital wickets for their teams.

Our recommendation to young cricketers is that they continue to develop versatility in their armoury. Surely, athletic batters can develop the skill to bowl orthodox spin with sufficient consistency to warrant inclusion in an attack at some point in time, even just to provide some relief for the specialists. A stronger case can be made for all players to develop their batting, since every player must bat in a game. All players should become competent in at least one fielding position without excuse. In the future, it might be productive to have fast bowlers who can turn to orthodox spin, like Colin Miller did for Australia at the end of his career? Why can't wicketkeepers work on their bowling and fielders practice some keeping so that another option is available to the captain?

Practise your specialty first and become an expert at your principal role in a team. Next, for a percentage of time, work on fielding in another position. Practice both offensive and defensive approaches to batting and bowling so that you can be depended on to adapt to any situation. If you are a fast bowler, see if you have any flair in bowling spin, and so on. Challenge yourself to add to your repertoire while still spending a lot of time on your specialty. Your team will reap the benefits.

Winning Premierships: The Ultimate Team Reward (Neil's Story)

I have been lucky in sport. In my impressionable years, I had a technical expert in George Murray, who taught me the skills of the game. When I was a little more mature, I had a hard taskmaster in former Australian vice-captain Keith Stackpole, who showed me the tougher side of the game. Intertwined with these two coaching doyens, I played alongside former Victorian star John Scholes and Ryder medalist John Douglas.

Of course, there were many others as well, all of whom contributed to my development as a player and as a coach. Along the way, I learnt what was required to be successful.

At 17 years of age, I played in the first of three successive premiership teams with my local baseball club, Coburg. This team contained three Australian players: John Swanson, Ron McIvor, and Alan McLean. I was also coached by baseball legend Lyn Straw. I quickly learnt the value of preparation, the need for excellence, and the importance of persistence. By age 21, in 1974, I was lucky enough to win the Helms award for the best player in the Australian championships, thanks mainly to the contribution of the successful people who helped guide me.

At 24, I decided to concentrate on cricket. With this decision, I also switched from the Fitzroy cricket club to the Carlton cricket club. In my first four years, we won three premierships. That meant I had played in six premierships in 10 years of top-level sport. Good fortune seemed to be following me.

By 32, I was offered the position of captain and coach of the Collingwood cricket club, a club with a proud history but little recent success. In the next eight years, we played in five grand finals, winning the premiership in the 1987-88 season. No doubt, something about success had been entrenched into me by the people with whom I had been so lucky to be involved.

As coach of the state under-19 team from 1995 through to 2004, the Victorian team won three championships. There were also runners-up another three times. Something was working!

The significance of all this is simple. If you wish to achieve success, surround yourself with successful people. In some cases, this is simply luck (being in the right place at the right time). However, in many cases, you can make the choice. In many situations, you can be the difference.

Over the years, I certainly learned the value of preparation, persistence, and trust. These qualities were ingrained into me by others, from my first coach to the star performers with whom I played. And although I never made the Australian cricket team, I at least did everything possible to reach my potential. No one can ask for any more. Most important, during my sporting journey I was involved in ten premierships. That's a good feeling, and it is within everyone's grasp.

Keith Stackpole								
	Matches	Inns	NO	Runs	HS	BT Ave	100s	Catches
Tests	43	80	5	2807	207	37.42	7	47
ODIs	6	6	0	224	61	37.33	0	1
First-Class	167	279	22	10100	207	39.29	22	166
List A	16	16	1	522	69	34.80	0	8

93

Kicking Goals to Launch a Season

I n order to set up the foundation of a cricket season, all members must make a collective effort to ensure that everyone remains on the same page throughout the year. Undertake the following steps to set a clear path for excellence.

Step One
Ask your players what they want from cricket. Most prefer to be successful, so look at areas where you have been short of the mark in previous seasons. Clearly, if the club wants to be successful, then change must be embraced.

Step Two
With all the stakeholders (players and committee), establish some values to drive the club. Self-discipline, teamwork, excellence, passion, courage, and preparation come to mind when assessing the qualities of successful teams. This takes a bit of time, but it is well worth the effort. The club performance can then be monitored in terms of these values. All stakeholders must have an understanding of the behaviours that underpin the values.

Step Three
Set up some training goals, such as the following:

- Make training fun, specific, purposeful, and intensive.
- Train at least as much as any other team in the competition.
- Monitor and reward attendance and effort at training.

Step Four
Establish club and team expectations related to match days. Examples include arrival time at a ground, warm-up procedures, and off-field duties when your team is batting.

Step Five

Establish a style of play and link it to the values.

Step Six

Look closely at the benchmark team in the competition to establish performance goals. Aim to replicate and better such results. Include all the components of the game: batting, bowling, and fielding.

Goals need to be specific, measurable, and challenging. They need to be visible and constantly reinforced by all at the club. If you launch every cricket season by kicking some goals, your score will mount rapidly.

94

Make Your Home Ground Away From Home

It has always puzzled us why pundits consider the home ground to be such a huge factor in predicting outcomes in sport. Sure, being familiar with the typical wickets at a particular venue does provide an inherent advantage. However, shouldn't this be a minor influence, compared to ability, fitness, smarts, and mental toughness? Have we started to believe in this notion so much that we go into an away contest expecting to lose?

Some core factors are common to every ground. The wicket will always be 22 yards long, the sun may or may not shine, the wind may or may not blow, and the bowlers will try to get your batters out. You need to plan for the peculiarities of any ground and their effect on performance. We believe that well-prepared athletes build up a store of information about different venues that will assist them to perform consistently when on an away wicket.

For example, if you were playing a game on the historically bouncy Western Australia Cricket Association pitch in Perth, you would be wise to practice ducking under any fast ball pitched in the bowler's half. Equally, you would need to make sure you are aware of the bounce from balls on a length that may cause nicks if diligent defence is not produced. Many players have made runs in their first innings at the WACA. It has typically been a great wicket for both batters and bowlers. Therefore, the policy should be to understand its unique nature and to adapt your game to accommodate to it. Similarly, the slope on the wicket at Lord's has unique characteristics to which batters need to adapt.

Keep data on the wickets you play on for your level of competition. A certain wicket may favour fast bowlers, while others favour spin. You may notice that a wicket produces a lot of leg before wicket decisions, which may indicate a tendency to keep low. Another pitch may produce a lot of wickets early on the first day, which may indicate more than the usual amount of moisture under the surface. Remember grounds that are typically fast or slow so that you can get some idea of a competitive tally for that ground.

It is useful also to train yourself to read wicket conditions so that you can learn to predict what they will be like when you get out to play. Make a habit of talking to opposition players about the condition of all grounds. These strategies will make you more familiar with the conditions so that you can perform at your peak. Being equally challenged by good and bad conditions will put you well on the way to having a home ground away from home.

What If Your Nightmares Come True?

S o often in my dreams, I have been engaged in combat at a high level in sport and have been frustrated by the outcome. Typically, these dreams prevent me from achieving my goal. Really, they are nightmares, because in my dream world I am thwarted by little obstacles. I am going out to bat but I don't have the right gear on; I have to do something other than play the most important game of my life; I have an atrocious practice session the day before, or someone asks me to change my game plan as I am going out to bat. In the classic dream, I am running away from some obscure invader. I awake so often from these nightmares feeling very upset with the fact that I am not in the environment I thought I was in!
(Ken Davis)

The reality of sport is that a host of situations can throw you off your game. Cricketers should prepare for all possible scenarios. Ask yourself 'what if?' Think of all the things that could happen to upset your preparation or performance. Work out a series of strategies that can assist you in overcoming them.

How would you handle the following possibilities?

- You have a bad practice session the day before a competition.
- You have experienced four successive failures in batting.
- You are asked to play a different role than you normally do.
- You are changed in the batting order as the game is in progress.
- You are losing a contest.
- You tend to panic when pressure is applied in competition.
- You are learning a new technique, but are making little progress.
- You have been publicly criticised by the coach.
- You are devastated after an unexpected loss in a crucial game.

- You have a negative attitude to playing away from home.
- You get dropped from the team.
- You are unable to perform well early in a contest.
- You bowl very well in first spells, but invariably perform below par later in the day.

The list could go on. The point we want to make here is that if you prepare for these circumstances, you will be better able to deal with them. As an exercise, consider each of the preceding scenarios and write down how you would respond to them.

Here is an example to set your pen in motion: Say you have a bad practice session just before competition. A positive response to this episode may include the following self-talk:

- 'That's good. I got that out of my system.'
- 'Not everything was bad. I am just going to focus on the good things I did.'
- 'The playing conditions will be different on match day, so I will just shrug off the session.'

Sometimes, it is worthwhile to finish your practice session on a good note. This might be as simple as having a few throw-downs in which you hit a few well-timed shots.

Preparing for your worst nightmare should be seen as a proactive step in developing strategies to combat any situation that occurs in competition. Soon, you will be so conditioned to respond in a positive manner to any adversity you meet, you might even hope another nightmare is just around the corner, ready to be conquered.

96

Boys to Men

The fact that young players are dropping out from our great game is a growing concern within cricket. In Australia, clubs have become proactive in attracting juniors to play through the highly successful program, Milo Have A Go. Similar programs exist throughout the world, ensuring that youngsters are exposed to cricket at an early age. Recruitment is important, but the retention of players may be a bigger issue.

Obviously, as children grow through their teenage years, a host of activities compete for their time. Is the dropout phenomena merely a reflection of these choices, or is it covering up complex factors within the sport?

The culture of cricket clubs (we hasten to add that we are referring to men's clubs) has often been based on a proclivity to overindulge in alcohol, treat women as sex objects, and spend copious hours telling yarns that border on the raunchy side of good taste. Clearly, we are overstating reality here. A lot of healthy fun and conviviality can occur at cricket clubs without venturing to extremes. However, we seek to make the point that the entry into a man's world may be daunting for a young boy who is nervously seeking his identity.

The easy way to deal with this anxiety is to join the masses and do as they do, etching more tales of young drunken behaviour into the folklore of the club. Do we have to rethink our values here? Should we be more inclusive and temperate in our social behaviour? Can we encourage families to become a part of a club that promotes fun and happiness in a responsible environment? Since cricket is now seen as an athletic endeavour, we should be encouraging all participants to lead healthy lifestyles.

Notwithstanding these social issues, young players must overcome other cricket-specific hurdles as they enter adult competitions. Typically, young players are targeted physically and verbally by their older counterparts. This can often be unpleasant and may decrease their enthusiasm for playing the sport. As they gain athletic skill, the barrage will subside in time. Young players are advised to hang in through this period.

The contest becomes even tougher in many respects as young players move up the grades. The loose ball becomes a rarity. Bowlers begin to subject the youngster's game to more scrutiny, searching for weaknesses. Experienced batters attempt to dominate a young bowler, particularly if he is a spin bowler. In order to work through this period, young players need to maintain strong self-esteem and remain very relaxed when they play. Knowing that this intimidation is likely to occur is an important step in handling it.

Young players often experience performance troughs when they enter the adult game. Since they are used to dominating a game, it takes them a while to adapt to the new level. Again, youngsters armed with this expectation are perhaps more able to cope with deterioration in their form. This natural process rarely escapes any young player.

Skilful coaches focus on the small details that make an elite cricketer. These are often neglected in junior ranks. Such an emphasis distances them from outcomes that may be less than satisfying at this time.

Clubs that are aware of potential problems are more likely to be able to guide youngsters through this period of turbulence. Hopefully then, youngsters may endure this time and maintain both a love for the game and a commitment to its future.

Body Language Tells a Story

From the minute you walk onto the field, you will convey an image. If you are nervous, you might be fidgety, rounding your shoulders a little and lowering your voice. Although this does not necessarily set you up for failure, the opposition will be all over you.

Batters should note the way that the top players stride to the wicket with an air of confidence. They are positive in their play, even when leaving a ball. They make loud and forthright calls. They back up aggressively, prepared to run. Even when they play and miss, they show no concern. They accept the mistake (or the good ball) and get on with business, using positive body language.

Bowlers must also assert themselves before and after a delivery. This does not have to be verbal, as some seem to think is necessary. You must approach the crease with decisiveness and confidence, letting the batter know that you mean business. Whatever happens after the delivery, you must be resolute with your actions. Don't complain about the outcome.

In the field, be active. Demonstrate your commitment to the defensive work by diving on the ball, running to back up as necessary, employing sharp throws to the wicketkeeper, and generally wanting to be part of the play, rather than hoping that the ball doesn't come to you.

Although positive body language will not improve your cover drive or make you bowl any faster, it just may give you a mental edge over your opposition. That one percent might be the difference between success and failure.

When David Beat Goliath (Ken's Story)

I n the late 1970s, I was fortunate to be named captain of a Victorian-country XI to play against the all-conquering West Indies team in the first game of their Australian tour. Our team consisted of country players who played cricket once per week in domestic cricket competitions. We had four players who had competed against Test players in the Melbourne premier cricket competition.

Our adversaries were clearly the most dominant team in the world at that time. They had an impressive array of fast-bowling options, and when I say fast, I mean lightning quick! Their batting boasted the master batsmen: Viv Richards, Gordon Greenidge, Desmond Haynes, Alvin Kallicharran, Clive Lloyd, and the pugnacious Larry Gomes.

This was a team that had no weakness. When our team was selected some three weeks prior to the game, I realised that it would be an experience we'd never forget. As the game approached, I feared that many of our players were excited about the experience, rather than any thought of challenging the best team in the world. I resolved to change that mentality. This was a contest between Mohammed Ali and Lionel Rose, Tiger Woods and the club champion at Casterton golf club, Michael Jordan and the best basketball player from Pomborneit. Let's face it, this was not meant to be a contest in the strict gladiatorial sense. We were supposed to get flogged, showcasing the talent of the West Indies in the name of promotion of the game in rural Victoria.

As we gathered for one of our three practice sessions before the game, I calmly addressed the players about the need to quicken up their reflexes to prepare themselves for a pace barrage, to get on the back foot to give themselves more chance to track the missiles projected by the Windies' attack.

This tour coincided with the introduction of protective headgear in cricket. Many players still believed it was a sign of weakness to wear such apparel. In fact, I'm sure some of the diehards regarded it as a form of cheating! Our club had purchased three helmets and encouraged players to use them, reasoning that it would give batters some confidence to get in behind the ball, which is a fundamental principle of the batting craft.

At practice for the Windies clash, I urged the players to trial the helmets. Most players found them uncomfortable and cumbersome. Some believed that their vision was impaired, while others felt that they couldn't play their strokes with their customary fluency. At the conclusion of the practice, only the players from my club (Michael Bowtell, Chris Lynch, and myself) were committed to wearing them. How was this to change? But I get ahead of myself.

As coach, I had to change the psychology of the group. I knew from the way the players were talking that, quite understandably, they rated the Windies as untouchables who were incredibly superior to us. However, I knew, having played premier cricket for a number of years and having batted against Test players, that the gap between reality and their imagination was nowhere near as great as they feared.

I started by convincing myself! 'I have made runs against Test players, so why can't these fellows do the same?' With renewed confidence, I called a meeting during the build-up to the game. My focus was to convince the players that on any given day, a rank outsider could defeat an odds-on favourite. History was full of such examples. I drew on some of these cases as I commenced my battle to change the team's thinking. I wrote 'How can we beat the Windies?' on the whiteboard. After reviving the players who fainted, we started to etch out a plan. I asked them to write down all that would have to happen for us to win. As you would expect, it took a while for the group to take this task seriously. Early responses indicated that our best chance rested on taking the scalpel to several intimate body parts of the opposition. In time, notions like these faded, and the players created the following game plan:

- The Windies would not take the game as seriously as a first-class game. They would be less prepared than normal.
- It was generally felt that we needed to restrict them to a score under 250. I thought it was unlikely that part-time cricketers could amass a big score against such quality bowlers.

- We would have to win the effort stakes, which meant dirty pants for everyone in the field. We would have to dive for the ball disregarding any thought of possible injury.
- Some players would have to do better than they had previously.
- We needed to be courageous and willing to take some blows on the body.
- Everyone would have to contribute.

I knew at the conclusion of that meeting that the seed had been sown. We knew we could beat the Windies.

The big day arrived under the cover of threatening skies. As I pressed the wicket for a photo with Clive Lloyd, I couldn't help but notice the size of his hands. He could fit my two hands in one of his! No wonder he could catch the ball with such nonchalance. As I walked off the field after winning the toss and sending the Windies in to bat, I had to fight the fear of inadequacy I felt after comparing myself physically to the athletic, dominant Lloyd.

We were pleased yet disappointed that the Windies left out Richards, Greenidge, Holding, and Garner. However, their pace attack of Croft, Marshall, and Roberts was still very formidable. Their batting contained a blend of stroke players, such as Haynes, Rowe, Kallicharran, Lloyd, and nudgers, such as Gomes. Predictably, we were shell-shocked at the start. All fielders found the ball reaching them before they expected it to. My shin at slip, after an edge from Haynes, was testimony to that!

In an hour of typical Windies aggression, they made 62 runs against our opening attack of David Beames and Andrew Scott. Most in the crowd had settled back to see the predicted domination of the fledglings from country Victoria. One towering six over square leg was a gentle reminder that these guys liked to hit the ball! Thankfully, as I cupped my hands at slip, the heavens opened up and play was abandoned for the day. Most suspected, like a killer on death row, that we were only granted a stay of execution.

In the afternoon, we arranged a game of golf with the Windies players. Strangely, this game gave me hope for the outcome of the cricket match. Chris Lynch and I were drawn to play with Desmond Haynes and the master blaster himself, Vivian Richards. Naturally, we were a little nervous on the tee. This was not helped by Desmond's first drive, which carried 280 metres straight up the middle. Then Viv stepped up, took a big swipe, and landed the ball amongst the eucalypts. He proceeded to go from tree to tree for much of the day. Even though we didn't play that well, we still had Vivvy covered at the end. This demonstrated to me that even the most gifted people have weaknesses. If Vivvy couldn't play golf all that well, then surely his team-mates would make some mistakes with the bat. We needed to be ready.

On day two we settled into our task more quickly, much like a footy final seems to settle after the frenetic first 10 minutes or so. I had opened with Andrew Scott bowling upwind and decided to give him a crack with the southwester at his back. Andrew was a likeable larrikin, always sporting a mischievous grin on his face. He was a typical, mad-fast bowler really, but quick and smart at his craft.

In what turned out to be a pivotal moment in the match, as I handed the ball to Andrew at the top of his mark, he said 'Be bold,' an obvious reference to one of the quotes I mentioned in our meeting pre-game. He proceeded to bounce the Windies with a sustained spell of hostile bowling. In no time at all, the Windies were 4-100 odd, and we had a game on our hands. Andrew had given us hope. Supported by improved fielding and some wily spin by Ian Treloar, we managed to dismiss the Windies for 224, on target!

Now, for the courage! Our leading player, Michael Bowtell, took strike against Colin Croft (who is 6 feet, 6 inches tall!). I guess we were wondering if they would bowl at something approaching top pace. Perhaps they might hold back and give us some half volleys. They might experiment with their swing. We watched in horror as the first ball was a searing bouncer that kept coming at Michael's helmet. He attempted to sway out of the path of the ball, but it thundered into his helmet and raced away for our first runs of the innings. They were here to play! Remember my earlier comments about our players' reluctance to wear helmets. Well, all of a sudden, the idea became more palatable to them. One by one, players filed down the steps and into the rooms to try on a helmet! 'Yeah, it's not so bad after all,' was the common call. If you had been a salesperson, you would have made a killing on that day. All of a sudden, $500 for a helmet seemed a good deal!

We lost Michael Bowtell cheaply and Peter Brady, a prolific run-getter from Ballarat, followed soon after. Chris Lynch looked terrific and got to 20 quite quickly before holing out. At 3-30, the writing was on the wall. Enter yours truly to partner Phillip Marshall. Phillip had been used to playing on the front foot on a flat wicket in Geelong. This was different. I took guard and peered at Malcolm Marshall, a speck on the horizon. He galloped in, shirt flapping in the breeze (as John Arlott, the doyen of cricket commentators, would say), and approached the crease with the conviction of a man at war. He gathered and flung this lethal cocktail in my direction.

I saw a blur in the soft twilight. The delivery was pitched short, so I went into autopilot and ducked. Alas, this was not the Western Australian Cricket Association wicket in Perth, with its pace and bounce. This was Geelong West, with disturbing unpredictability in bounce. The ball crashed into the back of my helmet. I must have been nearly leg before wicket as I tried desperately to limbo. 'Backfoot,' I said to myself, 'and be quick.' Somehow we survived to build a partnership. My back foot was nearly alongside the stumps! There was no way I was going to meet the ball! Phillip managed to spank a few drives and cuts interspersed with some unconvincing lobs just out of reach of fielders, when the ball was catapulted at his throat. We passed 50 and Phillip was gaining in confidence. I was just hanging in, unsure of the bounce. Eventually I was bowled by one that didn't rise a lot. Phillip confided later that it wasn't a good shot. I was thankful I was alive! 4-80 became 5-84, since Mark Seeckts went not long after me.

On day three, the warm-up was sloppy and the players were chatting away casually. Then, like the Marshall bouncer the previous day, it hit me. I called the players in. 'Hey, you don't think we can win do you? You've given up. All that needs to happen is that one guy needs to make 70, and the others have to chip in. I know you can make 70 (pointing to numbers 7 and 8), and I know you can make 20 (pointing to numbers 9, 10, and 11). Now, let's get back and prepare to win!' The edge returned. We lost an early wicket, but I liked the team's steely resolve.

Peter Caulfield, a handy late-order batter who was selected principally as the third seamer, strode to a fighting 69—one short of the target I had set! The others all chipped in with 15s and 20s. When David Beames stroked a ball through the covers, we moved to 225-9, and a lead on the first innings against the world champions.

Now, I doubt this feat rated a mention in the Guinness Book of Records, but it should have. I doubt whether Clive Lloyd remembers anything about the game at all. However, to 12 guys from rural Victoria, it was huge. It was the moment when we all learnt that no matter how good the opposition, on any given day, a David can beat a Goliath. Even as I write, I am starting to dream about playing and beating Tiger Woods at golf. I just have to do my best ever on one of his bad days, and I've got him. Never, ever give up!

99

Gaining Wisdom

Cricket wisdom can be gained from a variety of sources. Giving advice is not only the domain of the elite superstars of the game. Many intelligent, committed, and observant people play and watch the game without reaching the dizzy heights of representing their country.

So many experiences occur in every Australian summer that can provide learning opportunities for our future players. You can learn from watching both Test matches and the local under-12 competition. You can gain good advice from those who have taken block at Lord's or from those who have sent down a googly at Pomborneit. In short, cricket wisdom knows no boundaries.

The last section of this book aims to encapsulate this philosophy. The people involved are not all Test players. They are simply a collection of cricket aficionados who have devoted a lot of their life to playing and coaching cricket. We believe their advice and experiences can be helpful to all aspiring coaches and players.

99.05 Clinton Peake (Former First-Class Player and Australian Under-19 Captain)

Coaching Tip

Don't try to be someone else! I found it a great temptation to try to bat like other people I admired. I also had more success as a batsman by playing to my own strengths and game plan and ignoring what the batsman at the other end was doing. Staying true to my own strengths and personality has greatly assisted me at times of pressure to keep on doing what I think is right for me.

Advice for Players

Following the marketing of Twenty20 cricket and the one-day World Cup, I think a lot of young players fall into the trap of thinking they have to be able to score a run at every ball or be able to bowl every type of delivery in the book to be worth a game. The best advice I can give to a young player is that they must be able to do ordinary things extraordinarily well. Only by doing this will they be able to achieve and sustain above-average performance.

99.10 — Jason Bakker (Former First-Class Player)

Coaching Tip

Bat with selectivity and patience, knowing that scoring opportunities will always be nearby. Impatient and overzealous players tend to support their team-mates from the change rooms after they have thrown their wicket away.

Advice for Players

Train and aspire to be a complete player. Don't underestimate or undervalue other facets to the game of cricket apart from your core skill or competency. (I bet Phil Jacques wishes he spent more time on fielding practice at a younger age.)

99.15 — Belinda Clark (Former Australian Captain)

Coaching Tip

You will get out at some point, so make the most of the opportunity to score runs whilst you are in!

Advice for Players

If you consider your game as a bucket, the aim is to fill the bucket with as much targeted practice as you can at any early age. Those who have spent time filling their buckets will have a greater chance to be the best they can be.

99.20 Ben Oliver (Former First-Class Player)

Coaching Tip

Control the controllables. This concept took me from just playing the game to thinking about the game. It shaped my approach to training and preparation, and was also a valuable default setting for my thought process during a match.

Advice for Players

Understand your game and play to your strengths. Regardless of natural ability, players who fully understand what is required for them to perform at their best are in a better position to produce this in a match situation. An obvious extension of this is to play to your strengths, particularly at key moments in a match. By playing the shots or bowling the delivery that you are most comfortable with, you are more likely to produce a positive outcome.

99.25 Rohan Larkin (Former First-Class Player)

Coaching Tip

The best tip I got as a youngster didn't relate to technique, but to attitude. As a young A-grade player, I'd bowled a ball which reared off a length and hit the batsmen in the chest, which sent him moaning to the ground. With a 16-year-old boy's innocence and some genuine concern, I walked up to the batter and asked, 'Are you alright?' Hearing this, my captain marched me back to my mark. In amongst the abuse he gave me for showing concern for the health of the batsman was 'You're not out here to make friends.' Like all good captains, he sat me down after play and explained what he meant. The crux of it was that he was convinced that one of the main differences between an average player and a good player was sheer ruthlessness. Hence, if you injure an opposition player or make a few enemies amongst opposition players whilst endeavouring to give your absolute all for victory, then so be it.

Advice for Players

The best advice I'd give a player now is an old favourite. I would tell them that they must have 'CACCA,' which means courage, ability, character, commitment, and adaptability.

99.30 Ian Redpath (Former Australian Player)

Coaching Tip

I was always encouraged and coached to be positive, not always with stroke play, but with attitude. Hence, use positive footwork when attacking and defending. Tentative batting leads to trouble.

Advice for Players

Cricket is a lovely game and we all have ambitions to succeed and hopefully progress. You face two pressures in cricket: One is applied by the opposition and the other is applied by yourself. Try to play as well as you possibly can so that you are in the moment and your future will take care of itself. Many young players have great ambition, as one should have, but they are forever playing for the future rather than the present. What should be a great game turns into a nightmare.

99.35 David Hussey (Australian One-Day and Twenty20 Player)

Coaching Tip

The best piece of advice anyone ever gave me while growing up was 'No matter who is bowling, how fast, how good, how consistent, whatever the situation is, just watch the ball and everything will take care of itself.' Basically, this told me to trust my ability and technique and play on instinct. Most of all, it made me relax at the crease, because when I am relaxed, I play my best cricket. In the words of Rod Marsh, 'Cricket is such a simple game, don't complicate things.' The simple task of watching the ball is quite easy to achieve.

Advice for Players

The best advice I would give a young player is to always, always play for the team. Cricket can be such a selfish game, particularly when players just look after themselves. This disappoints me. However, if you always put your team-mates first, you will gain the respect within your team, and you will also become a better player by learning off your team-mates. Putting the team first is very rare, but it is such a valuable life skill to obtain.

99.40 Cameron White (Australian Test, One-Day, and Twenty20 Player)

Coaching Tip

'You are your own best coach.' I have always thought that was a good tip.

Advice for Players

As a young player, you will receive lots of advice and information from all types of people and coaches. Be prepared to listen to what people have to say about your game, particularly with respect to your technique with your batting, bowling, and fielding. Then, take it on board and decide what works best for you!

99.45 Brad Hodge (Australian Test Player)

Coaching Tip

Former Australian captain, Allan Border, once noted that when I made a 100, I seldom went on to make a bigger score. He said I needed to convert these scores into 170s to 200s. I then started to think bigger and plan to continue batting when I got past 100. Essentially, that is a mental challenge. You've conquered most bowlers by then, and the two dangers lurking are the second new ball and your own concentration. I learned to recognise the key moments of trouble ahead. If it was a tear-away fast bowler, I would think that at most I would probably have to face 15 balls in his spell, so I geared up to survive that test. Having survived that, so long as I respected other bowlers, they would not pose the same threat as the number-one strike bowler.

Advice for Players

Two things come to mind. The younger you master back-foot play, the quicker you will become a better player. Most 18-year-olds are front-foot players who have to learn back-foot play at that stage. That takes time. My advice is to learn back-foot play as soon as you can. Also, it is imperative that you practice hitting the ball naturally early on. Do not be overconcerned with technique. You should play a number of bat-and-ball activities to build up a natural, flowing hitting movement. I had a lot of that foundation in hitting skills before my dad started taking me to the nets as a 12-year-old, where I focused more on building a sounder technique in cricket.

99.50 Clea Smith (Victorian Spirit Player and Australian Representative)

Coaching Tip

Aim to be the best version of yourself, not the second-best version of somebody else. Being thrust into the senior Victorian team as a young, timid 18-year-old was extremely confronting. Overnight, my heroes had become my team-mates. What I had been aspiring to had become an expectation. The only way I knew how to achieve that was to emulate those who did it best. I was unaware of how this approach was putting limits on what I achieved. The day I recognised the difference between copying from my team-mates and learning from them, I gave myself the opportunity to reach my potential.

Advice for Players

If you love cricket, you'll love the challenges it brings. Passion will inspire success.

99.55 Nick Jewell (Victorian Opening Batsman)

Coaching Tip

The best piece of advice I have received as a player was to be prepared to play ugly. Find a way to succeed, find the style of game that works for you, and stick to it. It was vital for me when going from a middle-order player who used to like to play all the shots and attack when under pressure to being an opening bat in first-class cricket. Now I have a very simple game plan of good defence, a cut shot that is the main scoring shot. I try to work the ball off the hip or ribs to rotate the strike. It's simple, but it works for me.

Advice for Players

When challenged at a new level or going up a grade (4ths to 3rds, local cricket to premier cricket, or premier cricket to first-class cricket), don't play the bowler or his reputation; play the ball coming down the pitch. It is very easy to be dismissed by the bowler and not by the actual ball that was bowled!

99.60 — Rob Quiney (Victorian First-Class Player)

Coaching Tip

Keep it simple and enjoy your cricket.

Advice for Players

Listen to everyone, then sort through it and develop a game that suits you.

99.65 — Lloyd Mash (Victorian First-Class Player)

Coaching Tip

Always have a clear and open mind. Let your instincts take over.

Advice for Players

Approach every training session (skills or fitness) with the same intensity as you would in a game.

99.70 — Dirk Nannes (Victorian First-Class Player and Netherlands World Cup Player)

Coaching Tip

A good ball is a good ball to any player. It does not matter how good it is. For batting, when I was trying to hit it too hard one day, the tip was 'The ball only has to touch the fence, not break it.'

Advice for Players

Know what you are good at, and play to those strengths. If you can bowl a good bouncer, use it. If you can't bowl a yorker spot on 80 percent of the time, don't try one until you can do it in the nets.

99.75 — Kim Hughes (Former Australian Captain)

Coaching Tip

When batting, think 'head first, feet second.' So many coaches say 'Move your foot to the pitch of the ball.' My coach used to say the most important aspect of batting was to move your head toward where you wanted to play, and then the foot would follow. Hence, when playing an on drive, you move your head to the line of the ball first. In so doing, you avoid the problem of planting your foot to the off side and having to play around the pad in order to play a ball pitched on or outside leg stump.

Advice for Players

The day you are not having fun, it's time to give the game away. Always look forward to training and having some fun while working towards improving your game.

99.80 Darren Berry (Former Victorian Captain)

Coaching Tip

'The harder I work, the luckier I seem to get.' It's a bit of a cliché, but it's pretty good advice.

Advice for Players

Keep the main thing, the main thing.

99.85 Terry Alderman (Former Australian Swing Bowler)

Coaching Tip

One of the best tips I received was from Ray Lindwall after I had been selected for Australia. It concerned the amount of angle you put on the seam towards the slips to get the ball to swing out. His method was to hold the seam upright and straight, and use his wrist to create the angle to achieve the movement. It can be a bit complicated if you aren't already skilled in the art of swing bowling, so to be told this at my developed stage was perfect timing!

Advice for Players

A piece of advice I would give today to all players is that control is still your most important weapon, even if you're not getting movement with the ball. Keeping a consistent line and length and not giving free hits to a batter enables your skipper a chance to at least set a field for you. If you haven't got that control, work on it.

99.90 Sarah Elliot (née Edwards), Victorian Spirit Player and Australian Representative

Coaching Tip

Batting in cricket is a game of mathematics. You need to have the percentages in your favour when deciding on shot selection. If you can do something 90 percent of the time at practice, then to do that in a game is a low risk. Conversely, if you can only play a particular shot 10 percent of the time in practice, the odds are against you playing that shot successfully in a game.

Advice for Players

Each ball is an individual contest. The better you are at staying in the now, the better you will perform.

 ## 99.94 You!

What wisdom can you add?

About the Authors

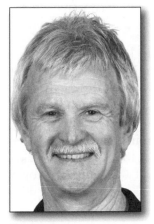

Ken Davis

Neil Buszard

Both Ken Davis and Neil Buszard have devoted much of their lives to playing and coaching cricket. Both played and coached high-level grade cricket in Australia, coached state representative teams, and represented Australia. Neil was a player with the Australian baseball team and Ken was coach of the Australian youth women's team. Both batted high in the order, bowled leg spin, and were more than competent fielders.

With a background in teaching, it was inevitable that both authors would be attracted to coaching cricket. Both coached players for many years, guiding their teams to achieve consistent success.

Neil moved from teaching to become the head coach of cricket at the Victorian Institute of Sport in 1995, where he spent the next 12 years. In that period, the Victorian U19 team (of which he was coach for 10 years) won three national titles. They were runners-up on another three occasions. Graduates of Neil's innovative and balanced program have become elite cricketers, and many have made their mark in other fields, including cricket administration. Neil's ability to develop people skills as well as cricket skills sets him apart from many coaches. His unbridled enthusiasm for the game, coupled with his energetic and thoughtful approach to performance enhancement, has long placed him at the forefront of coaching in Australia.

As a player, he played more than 300 games of premier cricket. A division of the Victorian premier cricket competition was named in his honour during the 2006-07 season. He was also a very successful baseball player, representing Australia as a third baseman and winning the coveted Helms award for the best player in Australia.

Neil has always encouraged and valued his support staff. Merv Hughes (Australian test selector), Darren Berry (Victorian captain and now assistant state coach), Ben Oliver (International Cricket Council development manager for south-east Asia), and Simon Helmot (Victorian Academy coach) are just some of the people who would class Buzz as a significant mentor in their coaching and professional development.

Ken's academic pursuits took him to Perth in 1972, where he completed a master's degree in physical education. His thesis, entitled *A cinematographic analysis of fast bowling in cricket,* was the catalyst for more than 30 years of research of this explosive and often potentially harmful motion in our sport.

During this time, in Perth, he played a part in Subiaco's two premierships in three seasons. The first was under the control of world-renowned coach Daryl Foster, and the second was under his own direction against a Perth side that included the famous duo of Dennis Lillee and Rod Marsh.

Ken worked with Frank Pyke and Gary Crouch to develop a successful rehabilitation program for Lillee after his much-publicised back injury. After returning from Perth, Ken continued to develop his coaching skills at the Essendon and Geelong cricket clubs whilst also lecturing at Deakin University.

In 1989, he completed a PhD in sport psychology from Florida State University in the United States. He has subsequently worked with a number of elite athletes and teams in the role of sport psychologist, most notably with the Geelong and Richmond football teams in the Australian Football League.

For the past 10 years, Ken has worked full time at Cricket Victoria in a variety of roles, including coaching the Victorian Spirit women's team to two national titles and two second-place finishes in five seasons. He also led the Australian women's youth team in successful tours of New Zealand and Sri Lanka.

Ken and Neil have both been heavily involved in coaches' education in Victoria for more than 30 years. Ken has published a number of articles in referee and professional journals, and both have presented at national and international conferences in cricket, sport science, and related areas.

Both authors had mentors in their early years. Ken believes George Tribe, who coached him at University C.C., was the most influential in transforming his view of cricket from a pastime to a science. His supportive, sport-loving family encouraged him to explore his passion.

Neil also had tremendous family encouragement. He drew many of his coaching philosophies from former vice-captain of Australia's cricket team Keith Stackpole, legendary youth coach George Murray, and Australian baseball coaches David Went and Lyn Straw.

The authors strongly believe that good cricket coaches can come from a number of backgrounds. Some excellent coaches were outstanding players, but just as many were good players who linked a thirst for learning with the wisdom of their experience and sport science. The authors of this book fall into the latter category. We hope you enjoy their work.